Building Strategic Relationships

William Bergquist
Juli Betwee
David Meuel

Building Strategic Relationships

How to Extend Your Organization's Reach Through Partnerships, Alliances, and Joint Ventures

Jossey-Bass Publishers • San Francisco

Substantial discounts on bulk quantities of Jossey-Bass books are available to corporations, professional associations, and other organizations. For details and discount information, contact the special sales department at Jossey-Bass Inc., Publishers. (415) 433–1740; Fax (800) 605–2665.

For sales outside the United States, please contact your local Paramount Publishing International office.

TCF Manufactured in the United States of America on Lyons Falls Pathfinder Tradebook. This paper is acid-free and 100 percent totally chlorine-free.

Library of Congress Cataloging-in-Publication Data

Bergquist, William H.
    Building strategic relationships: how to extend your organization's reach through partnerships, alliances, and joint ventures/William Bergquist, Juli Betwee, David Meuel.
      p.cm.—(The Jossey-Bass management series)
    ISBN 0-7879-0092-3
    1. Strategic alliances (Business) 2. Interorganizational relations. 3. Partnership. 4. Joint ventures. 5. Consortia.
I. Betwee, Juli, date. II. Meuel, David, date. III. Title.
IV. Series.
HD69.S8B47 1995
658'.044—dc20
                                      94-46746

HB Printing   10 9 8 7 6 5 4 3 2 1   FIRST EDITION

Contents

Preface

There is nothing new about partnerships. For centuries, people in every conceivable line of work have been forming them. More than 2,500 years ago, the Greek city-states formed mutual-defense pacts to beat back invasions from Persia. The pyramids of ancient Egypt—long thought to be the grand achievement of an elaborate hierarchy—were actually the result of quite sophisticated partnership arrangements. We could, in fact, trace the concept of partnering all the way back to the creation of the first family unit.

But for many people, partnerships—especially in business—represent a great unknown. For much or most of their adult lives they have worked in hierarchical organizations. Even professional partnerships, best known in the fields of accounting, law, and medicine, are formed and staffed on a hierarchical model. For the most part, members of these organizations are separated into the professionals and the nonprofessionals, the leaders and the led, those who give orders and those who take them. The kind of partnerships forming today, based not so much on legal considerations as on collaboration and trust, have seemed too risky, too intimidating to attempt until the present.

Partnering is a discouraging experience for some. People are attracted to the widely touted benefits of partnering, such as the ability to share expertise, leverage precious R&D dollars, or gain access to new markets. They're intrigued by the talk of strategic alliances, virtual corporations, joint ventures, consortia, and the many other fascinating partnership forms popularized in recent years. But when they take the plunge, they find themselves or their partners ill prepared for or ill suited to the challenge.

Yet, for a growing number of people, partnerships exceed their greatest expectations. Companies large and small have found great benefits in the approach. And not only have the individuals involved helped their organizations succeed but they have also benefited in other, more personal ways. "You think differently about the people you work with," one financial industry executive confided to us. "Your working relationships are more positive overall. People seem happier. It's a much more pleasant situation in which to work."

The reason for the growing interest in public and private partnerships and the attention they're receiving in the business press is obvious: the world is changing in ways that make partnerships more important, if not essential, to achieving success in virtually every kind of professional endeavor. Partnerships simply represent a better way to do things. The current emphasis on close strategic relationships contrasts with the merger wave that formed the octopuslike conglomerates of the 1960s. The prevailing wisdom at that time was that an amalgamation of unrelated businesses would provide a hedge against fluctuating profits in its individual components. That period also marked the peak of faith in modern professional managers. It was believed that these managers, using similar sets of skills, could run any type of business, from retail clothing stores to computer companies. In addition, people held to the notion that the bigger the company, the more attractive it would be to the best and brightest new talent.

In the 1970s it was fashionable to invest in diversified portfolios made up of stock in companies with a common focus. Following that rule, ITT, a paradigm of 1960s-style conglomeration, subsequently spun off many of its disparate business lines. And LTV, another one of the large conglomerates of the period, has gone bankrupt. Conversely, AT&T, the giant telecommunications monopoly, began spinning off its businesses as independent units that have become, in today's expanding market, fierce competitors. The market trend in the 1980s was to follow an approach opposite to conglomeration. The favored technique was the leveraged buy-out: purchase a company from its shareholders and sell the assets, betting that individually the value of the pieces will be worth more than the whole.

The strategic relationships being established today—called by such names as partnerships, joint ventures, licensing agreements, and the like—are forming whole new industries (like interactive media) and creating new technologies (like bioengineering). They represent efforts to combine the best available resources, to take advantage of openings in a global marketplace, and to add value in unbounded enterprises.

Partnering is currently getting the most notice in the telecommunications, computer, and entertainment industries. Medical care, a business that for years passed on price increases to its customers without much thought, is now facing a consumer revolt. Drug companies, hospital chains, and health maintenance organizations are scurrying to consolidate, in an effort to whittle away at operating costs by forming alliances with each other to increase market penetration.

Although fewer and fewer of us are working for corporate giants, many such organizations are bellwethers of dramatic shifts in the marketplace. Time Warner Inc. and US West are delivering an increasing array of entertainment and telecommunications services. AT&T and General Magic are developing "smart messaging," where messages are delivered through a sophisticated series of networks. To illustrate how single entrepreneurs can join up with larger concerns, consider the formation of General Magic, the result of a relationship between some former Apple employees and Sony, Matsushita, and Motorola. Intel and MCI are blending personal-computing and long-distance phone technology. Ford Motor Company has plans to build a universal car, one that's suitable for a global market. This sort of "mass customization" will certainly require global partnerships in order to work.

We must replace "or" with "and" in order to become necessarily inclusive in our thinking and actions—to keep up with the changing boundaries within and between people, organizations, and industries. As organizations redefine their businesses and spawn new industries in response to external changes in the marketplace, they develop new institutional identities. Postmodern organizations rediscover themselves internally, and they force us to rethink how our entire system of stakeholders works. Business, which was at one time defined by internal functions and boundaries, now includes the ultimate consumer, vendors and suppliers, competitors, employees, the community it serves, and other external sources. And the strength of this new system is closely tied to the strategic health of its businesses and industries.

The rate of change in our businesses and society in general is accelerating, variable, and paradoxical (Bergquist, 1993). We are leveraging growth in a downsized environment. We used to think of power in terms of size. We now think of power in terms of quality, information, and the relationships required to do the work. We are beginning to emphasize *predicting* financial performance, using both hard and "soft" sociological metrics, realizing that to look solely at hard outcomes as measures of success is to look too late in the game. Organizational learning and product quality—as defined by the end user—are not typically discernible in hard tangible outcomes, yet they are clearly becoming competitive advantages.

Globalization is happening in our external and internal markets. Diversity is as apparent in our consumer mix as it is in our labor mix. Globalization and diversity are mirrors of each other. Diversity in our organizations will help us to better understand the buying habits of our customers. This phenomena is more a function of mind-set than of geography.

There is a tremendous amount of shifting and blurring of our boundaries, roles, and markets. Look at the financial services market. We can do banking almost any place and time these days. In many cases competitors share information or even become each other's customers. In short, there is less time and capital available to do what we used to do on our own, as autonomous businesses. We are being forced to form partnerships in order to survive. The permanence that used to define security, in employment and business relationships, is no more. Thus the stage is set for virtually all of us in positions of leadership in contemporary organizations to consider, at least once and often many times, the formation of a partnership with one or more other organizations.

While much has been written about professional partnerships in recent years, many people still seem ill prepared for the experience. Even highly trained executives concede that "Partnering 1-A" was not part of the curriculum in business school. Even successful partners talk frequently about "groping around in the dark" and "the blind leading the blind." Perhaps the best analogy we can use to describe the experience is that of courtship and marriage.

The Purpose of the Book

After an initial review of the writings about partnership and a number of consultations with business leaders and other consultants, we saw that, while much of value has been written on the subject, several critical issues are rarely discussed and several key questions rarely asked, let alone answered. First, we felt that not nearly enough has been said about the actual personal and organizational experience of being in a partnership. Many articles, for example, mention that trust is an essential component of a partnership. But often this is placed in a sidebar titled something like "Five Ingredients for Success" and limited to an item in a bulleted list: "Find partners you can trust." Rarely do we see the subject treated in the depth we believe necessary. Rarely, for example, do we hear extended testimony from partners sharing their insights on why trust is essential and how it can be built up or torn apart.

Second, we found that while much has been written about creating partnerships, relatively little attention has been paid to the process of maintaining and, when necessary, changing the terms of partnerships. How do partnerships fare on a routine, day-to-day basis—years after the excitement of formation? What needs to happen for partnerships to adapt to changing conditions? When is it appropriate to end a partnership? And how can partners do this constructively? We felt that these questions needed to be asked and addressed in a substantive way.

Third, we found that, while we constantly hear about partnerships between giants like GM and Toyota or about people leaving their corporate jobs to form small partnerships with ten or less people, we rarely hear about the midsized partnerships. Numbering in the thousands, these include businesses that come together to share resources and gain access to benefits too costly to get on their own, joint ventures and alliances that form to gain access to new markets, and supplier-customer relationships that add value for the end consumer.

From the outset we surmised that, whether partnerships are large or small, there are characteristics common to all of them. All, for example, face common challenges when they are created, when they face change from within, and when they face change from the outside. We believed that a document of these common challenges and the ways they are faced would be valuable to people considering either entering a partnership or changing the way they operate in one.

Finally, we came to identify very strongly with the sentiments expressed by the financial industry executive we quoted earlier: partnerships really can change the way people work together and the way they perceive each other, and they allow businesses to add value and a competitive advantage in today's marketplace. Partnerships offer a great potential as a humanizing and ultimately liberating force in our society.

The Case Studies

With all this in mind, we began the process of identifying and developing case studies of partnerships, both from our own interviews and from existing literature. Over a three-year period (1991–1994), fifty students from two graduate schools in the San Francisco Bay Area (the Professional School of Psychology and the School of Management at John F. Kennedy University) conducted more than two hundred interviews and compiled seventy-five case studies with regard to partnerships. While some of these case studies concerned small, family-based partnerships (to be used in a forthcoming book), many concerned medium-sized, interorganizational partnerships.

We have made extensive use of forty of these case studies and have included anecdotal material from twenty-five others. In addition, Juli Betwee conducted three sets of interviews with the leaders of several organizations involved in multiple partnerships. These three case studies are treated in depth in Part Three. We have also incorporated insights from our own personal experiences, from our consulting work, and from our teaching.

While our focus has been on intercompany partnerships, in today's world it is often difficult to know where one company's boundaries begin and another's end, and who learns what from whom. We have explored, with special interest, the human aspects of partnership. We see partnerships as living systems, and we have looked for the themes and patterns that make up their multidimensional relationships. We believe this web of relationships is the essence of an organization's sustained health and its ability to remain competitive in today's changing global environment.

Overview of the Contents

To explore the experience of partnership in the necessary depth and detail, we devoted the first chapter to defining the context in which today's partnerships exist. Because partnerships represent a new paradigm for business, a trend more substantial than just another fad, we wanted to begin by addressing these questions: Why now? Why partnerships? And how does the emergence of partnership structures represent a broad social—perhaps even global—trend? The second chapter focuses on the nature of partnership and addresses two central questions: How are partnerships different from and better than hierarchies for today's world? What are the key features of successful partnerships, based on the existing literature in the field and on our own consulting experiences?

In Part Two we trace what we discovered from our interviews regarding the developmental stages of a partnership. Since the metaphor of romance and relationships seems the closest—and certainly the most widely used—for partnerships, we've used it as well in tracing the life of partnerships. We have a hunch that what many of us have experienced in our personal lives—coming to terms with false expectations about marriage for life, living with dual roles, and confronting blurred gender and ethnic boundaries—have been precursors to what is happening in the business world. In a recent article *Fortune* magazine (February 21, 1994) referred to "hard-nosed businessmen's use of embarrassingly romantic terms to describe the new order in supplier-customer relationships. . . . 'It's like marriage,' croons a big-league purchasing executive. Says a less sentimental top industry manager: 'Its like committing to one relationship instead of sleeping around'." We've grouped the partnership experience into three developmental stages. Chapter Three focuses on the first stage: the courtship. The second stage, commitment, is described in Chapter Four; it focuses on living with the partnership. In Chapter Five we examine transformations in partnerships—including shifting the nature of partnerships and bringing partnerships to an end.

In Part Three we explore three specific partnerships in some depth. One of these case studies is the focus of Chapter Six. It is a supplier-customer partnership between a newspaper publishing company (Lesher Communications) and a newsprint supplier (Norpac). The second case study, in Chapter Seven, is a joint venture between Arthur Andersen, a worldwide accounting and consulting firm, and a California school system, the Alameda Unified School District (AUSD). The third, which we describe in Chapter Eight, exists as a consortium of companies—The Council for Continuous Improvement (CCI)—spanning multiple industries, countries, and sectors coming together to share information about their business and organizational processes.

We then take these cases, as well as our interviews and review of the literature, into Part Four, where we ask what we learned about partnerships. Using examples from real life, we test some of our early hypotheses: Why partnerships? How are they different? What are the essential components?

In Chapter Nine we focus on the central ingredient of any successful partnership—that is, the nature of the commitment that has been made by the partners. We distill the essence of effective partnerships by describing the partnership commitment as a relationship based on a covenant rather than a contract—as an organizational structure that requires trust in competency, intentions, and shared perspectives and values. In Chapter Ten we offer some lessons to guide your own decisions regarding partnership and some tools to help you assess where you are and what to expect at different stages of partnering.

Acknowledgments

We wish first of all to thank the men and women who offered to discuss their partnership experiences with us and our students. While we have preserved their confidentiality by disguising their identity, we want them each to know how valuable their insights and observations have been to us. Partnership ventures often go beyond the walls of their respective organizations to yield tangible results—and heartaches—for all parties. We have had the privilege of reflecting on these ventures through the experiences of visionary people who have encountered the challenges and problems and found new ways of working together. People who tell their partnership stories come from business, government, and education; from large organizations and small ones; and from successful partnerships and from ones that fell far short of expectations.

Second, we want to express our appreciation to the students who conducted these interviews. While they have been acknowledged elsewhere (a list of case-study contributors follows The

Authors) we want specifically to note their competence and their commitment to completing this demanding project.

Third, we wish to acknowledge all the people who contributed their time and information to building our three in-depth case studies and their experience and wisdom to this collaborative enterprise. Major contributors were Don Jochens and the employees at Lesher Communications and their partners at Norpac and at Weyerhaeuser Corporation. Nancy Clark, Tom Kelly, Mort Egol, and Richard Measelle are to be acknowledged for their pioneering work with their School of the Future at Arthur Andersen. We also acknowledge the early innovators in the Alameda Unified School District, who are rethinking education. Our thanks to Pat Reilly, Pete Hamm, and Bob Turnbull affiliated with the Council for Continuous Improvement, who are challenging mind-sets regarding how we compete in American business.

Fourth, we appreciate the contributions made to this book indirectly by our clients and colleagues who are collectively exploring and bringing new meaning to the complex web of relationships that are at the essence of the health and sustainability of contemporary organizations.

Finally, a deeply felt sense of gratitude must be extended to several individuals in our lives who have not only made this book possible but have themselves taught us much about the nature of partnerships. We specifically wish to thank our spouses—Kathleen O'Donnell, Michael Doyle, and Barbara Toothman—and our parents—Victor and Francis Bergquist, Vicki and Marc Betwee, and Charles and Harriett Meuel. They have all offered us the wisdom of collaborative work.

As we observed and wrote about partnerships in preparing this book, the three of us often wondered about the depth of the trend and how it is represented in other aspects of our lives and other parts of the globe. Through our work we learned that there is a much greater possibility for partnerships than we initially considered. Not only can they be key to achieving success in professional

endeavors but they can form a blueprint for deeper and more intimate ways of working together in the human relationships we share
while we work. We hope that this book contributes to this expanded sense of partnership and the role it can play in creating a
more fulfilling world.

March 1995

William Bergquist
Tiburon, California

Juli Betwee
San Francisco

David Meuel
Palo Alto, California

The Authors

William Bergquist has been an active organizational consultant and teacher for more than thirty years, having worked in Asia and Eastern Europe as well as North America. From 1986 to 1994, he served as president of the Professional School of Psychology, with campuses in San Francisco and Sacramento, California. He received his B.A. degree (1962) in psychology from Occidental College and his M.A. degree (1965) and Ph.D. degree (1969), also in psychology, from the University of Oregon, Eugene.

From his early interest in social psychology and the psychology of religion to his more recent interest in profound institutional and societal change, Bergquist has consistently puzzled over and consulted on the issues of freedom, the balancing of rights and responsibilities, and the nature of authority. He has addressed these issues in several books, including *The Postmodern Organization: Mastering the Art of Irreversible Change* (1993) and, with Berne Weiss, *Freedom: Narratives of Change in Hungary and Estonia* (1994). He is currently writing a book about the role of sanctuaries in our turbulent postmodern world.

Juli Betwee works in business and industry as an organizational consultant. She is a partner with HRMG and is chairwoman of Michael F. Doyle and Associates. Both are international consulting firms based in San Francisco, with affiliate offices in Paris. Betwee earned her B.A. degree (1969) in psychology at Michigan State University and her M.A. degree (1971) at Wayne State University.

Her career has focused primarily on the human and organizational dynamics of change in today's business world. She has had twenty years' experience working with emerging technology and Fortune 500 companies, both as an internal consultant and an external change agent. Her deep interest in partnerships grew out of her personal experience as a woman in a society largely dominated by win/lose competition, hierarchical structures, and paternalistic organizational cultures. She has a concern for bringing the qualities of community, honesty, dignity, and love into our business lives. She sees partnerships as the key to creating true high-potential organizations, more strategically positioned to perform in today's global economy.

David Meuel works as an independent promotional writer specializing in executive speeches for high-technology and financial services corporations. He earned his B.A. degree (1972) in English at the University of California, Davis, and his M.A. degree (1973) in English at the University of Michigan, Ann Arbor. He has also worked as a writer for KTEH-TV, a PBS affiliate in San Jose, California, and Advanced Micro Devices, an integrated-circuit manufacturer headquartered in Sunnyvale, California.

Since going into business for himself in 1983, Meuel has written hundreds of speeches for more than eighty different business executives and government officials, including the CEOs of four Fortune 500 companies and a State of California cabinet secretary. His interest in organizational partnerships grew out of his experiences writing about the subject for many of these people.

Meuel's additional professional credits include publication of more than seventy magazine and newspaper articles and more than two dozen poems, production of a full-length stage play, and recognition in six national playwriting and poetry competitions.

Case-Study Contributors

Mary Ann Beaumont

Kelly Daniels

Kim Detiveaux

Angela C. Di Berardino

Judy Harrower

James F. Knickerbocker, Jr.

Brad A. Lawrence

Janice Loomis

Gerald McGourty

Diane M. Meads

B. J. Metas

Jane Jernigan Michel

Patrick Reilly

Don Reynolds

Jim Rourke

Carolyn Teresa

Jeff Tomeo

Charlotte Toothman

Building Strategic Relationships

Part One

Thriving in an
Interdependent World

Chapter One

The Growing Need for Collaboration

When you're through changing, you're through.
—*American Saying*

Beginning in the late 1970s and early 1980s, a major change occurred in business computing. The traditional computer pyramid, consisting of a centralized mainframe, minicomputers, personal computers, and low-level "dumb" terminals, was crumbling. In its place a new, nonhierarchical model was taking shape. In this "distributed" approach, high-powered desktop workstations were seamlessly networked with even more high-powered information "servers." Rather than flowing downward, like a waterfall, information flowed sideways, from peer to peer. It swirled about the network like the currents in a whirlpool.

According to the advocates of distributed computing, this change represented a fundamental upheaval in the way organizations share and assimilate information. It is a more "egalitarian" scheme, they say, one that offers faster and freer data flow and easier and more widespread access to information. This fundamental shift in how we circulate information and derive meaning has transformed how we live and work. Indeed, the advent of technology in general has enabled nothing short of a revolution. Knowledge has become a form of currency and a new source of capital. The advent of technology has given birth to the knowledge-based revolution.

The Winds of Change

While profound in their own right, the changes brought about by computers are only a part of the even more dramatic and far-reaching changes apparent in the world around us. The speed and intensity of change that we witness almost daily on a global scale has become both persistent and unpredictable. Change, as defined by author and consultant Peter Vaill (1989), is like permanent white water. It is rapid, constant, and recurring. The pace of change in today's world is both driven by and the result of the knowledge revolution and its enabling technologies.

Boundaries as we knew them in modern society are now blurring (Jameson, 1991). Almost everywhere we look, our definition of turf is up for grabs. We are told (and see evidence to support it) that the nation-state is giving way to tribes and newly formed geopolitical communities. Redrawing the lines on what once seemed a semipermanent map of our world is like drawing in the sand. From the birth of the European Community in the 1960s to the reunification of Berlin in 1990; from the powerful alliances forming among the Tigers and Dragons of East Asia to the new coexistence of Israel and Palestine, boundaries that once steadfastly defined economies, societies, industries, companies, employees, and even genders are being redrawn, rethought, reengineered, and transformed. Boundaries were once drawn by others; now we speak about defining our own personal boundaries based on mutual trust and commitment.

The new, global context has become the expanded framework for defining our world. In addition to actually traveling around the globe, we can now also "surf" the airwaves to communicate, face to face, with any part of the world where there is access to a satellite dish. Paradoxically, as we open up our access to the people and experiences of the world in which we live, we become more focused on our local actions and our individual relationships. Bridging the similarities and differences in our transnational and *transcultural* world has become one of the biggest challenges of the global marketplace. A whole new competitive stage has just been set.

These major, external trends mirror another trend in recent organizational life: the gradual erosion of hierarchies and the emergence of more collaborative, partnership-driven structures. This is not to say, of course, that all hierarchies are going the way of the dinosaurs and the buggy whip manufacturers. Military organizations throughout the world are virtually unanimous in their claim that one of their great strengths lies in a clearly delineated chain of command. One of the world's oldest hierarchies, the Roman Catholic Church, shows little sign of willingly changing its basic structure. And, while much attention has been given to emerging business partnerships, most businesses will remain—at least to some extent—hierarchical. The layers of management will be reduced, more authority will be delegated throughout the organization, and greater reliance will be placed on outside resources. But the basic pyramid of power—albeit in a flatter, more fluid form—is unlikely to erode.

From Pyramid to Partnership

What *is* happening, however, is a giving way, a lessening of the hold that hierarchical structures have had over businesses, governments, educational institutions, nonprofit groups, and organizations of all kinds. One by one, people are turning their eyes outward. One by one, they're seeing how *other* people and organizations can help them to achieve key goals more efficiently and effectively. And one by one, they are creating new structures that are more collaborative, more egalitarian, and more flexible in nature: structures in which people view themselves as a part of a whole, complex system; structures in which the whole is greater than the sum of its parts.

In recent years large- and medium-sized companies have been at the forefront of this movement. Confronted with growing pressure to "do more with less," responding to the quickening pace of change, and taking advantage of new opportunities in foreign markets, businesspeople have looked at their often tired, lumbering hierarchies with fresh, critical eyes. Their response has frequently been to review, rethink, and reorganize—to "reinvent themselves," as the management books like to say. In the process, they have questioned the ongoing feasibility of their multitiered, vertically integrated companies. And they have adopted—or invented—a plethora of new partnership-based structures: cross-licensing agreements, strategic alliances, hollow partnerships, virtual partnerships, vertically integrated partnerships, and consortia (all of which we will more fully describe in Chapter Two). The list of terms used to describe these new, more collaborative and partnership-oriented organizational models doesn't stop here, of course. Other terms frequently heard range from "internal networks" to "compact agencies." And no doubt new terms will continue to be coined.

As we see it, this partnership phenomenon encompasses a myriad of forms. We believe, however, that they all follow similar patterns in how they come together, define their relationships, and manage transitions. These common threads apply to small businesses as well as to those that are large- and mid-sized.

A promotional writer and graphic designer we interviewed talked about their partnership, an informal arrangement they call a "virtual agency." Each has his own business, and the two join forces only when there is a need to work together to develop corporate marketing pieces, from brochures to advertisements. One of their great assets is their ability to offer "genius for less." Because they are not a traditional ad agency, with three layers of management, expensive office space, and an ornate conference room complete with a wet bar, they operate with far less overhead. Because they do the work themselves, clients are assured it won't be delegated to a writer or designer they've never met. Often these smaller, hands-on firms can provide better, more tailored services for less money. And they're giving the bigger, cost-laden agencies and professional-service firms a run for their money.

Private businesses have by no means been alone in seeking out and forging partnerships. In recent years, new and often quite creative alliances have proliferated in the public sector as well. In 1982, for example, former U.S. president Jimmy Carter joined forces with Emory University in Atlanta to form the Carter Center. Located on Emory's campus, the center is a private, nonpolitical organization that works to resolve international conflicts as well as to help people improve the quality of their lives during peacetime. One of the many ways the center and the university combine their resources for mutual benefit is through a special group called the International Negotiation Network, or INN, which is part of the Carter Center. With much of the work done by Emory students, the INN studies potential and ongoing conflicts around the world and ways to prevent or end them. In addition, some of these students are invited to attend peace conferences at the center (Carter, 1993).

In San Francisco a group of twenty-one people came together in the late 1980s to form a nonprofit organization called Coleman Advocates for Children & Youth. The group, which includes a day-care teacher, a nun, a police officer, an ex–Peace Corps volunteer, a lawyer, and a few homemakers, came together out of a shared concern for the welfare of children in the city. Together they put together a voter referendum to require San Francisco's city charter to guarantee that children receive their fair share of funding in the annual city budget. Despite skepticism from elected officials and the local chamber of commerce, they gathered sixty-eight thousand signatures on petitions to put the measure on the ballot, went on talk shows, talked to more than one hundred neighborhood groups, and enlisted the help of hundreds of other ordinary people. Then, on November 5, 1991, the voters responded, making San Francisco the first American city to guarantee funding for children each year in its city budget (Brodkin, 1993).

In Denver, the Colorado Symphony Orchestra has transformed itself into a musical cooperative. A traditionally structured (and debt-ridden) symphony for years, the CSO reached a crisis point in 1989. More than $5 million in debt, it tried to cut its musicians' pay by two-thirds. The musicians rebelled, walking out and signing with a local promoter to do a concert series. But the musicians weren't very successful on their own, and so they agreed to work with the

CSO trustees to form a new entity. The two most apparent strengths of the new CSO, insiders agree, are its tight fiscal controls and its much more cooperative structure. The old seventy-five-member board, filled with pillars of the Denver establishment, was replaced with a new twenty-seven-member board, which included nine musicians elected by their peers. This new structure has allowed the musicians to become more familiar with the promotional and fund-raising aspects of the business. And they often help make programming decisions with an eye to broadening CSO's appeal. As a result, the CSO has largely shaken its once-stuffy image—and its debt. In 1993 its ticket sales were up 50 percent, and it was making a small surplus (Atchison, 1993).

In addition, a large number of consortium-type partnerships have emerged that join private- and public-sector organizations. In June 1993, for example, the newly formed Consortium for Supplier Training, an alliance of seven companies (including Motorola, Xerox, Kodak, and Digital Equipment Corporation), turned over its in-house courses on benchmarking and other proven quality control methods to select community colleges nationwide. Now the schools teach the courses to the suppliers of consortium members— and anyone else who wants to take them. While a handful of schools currently participate, the consortium members have great hopes for expansion. "Our vision," confides James R. Partner, manager of supplier quality for Xerox, "is to have hundreds around the country involved" (Therrien, 1993, p. 76).

Increasingly, too, the size and scope of these private- and public-sector partnerships can be immense. In September 1993, for example, the U.S. government and the Big Three U.S. automakers, GM, Ford, and Chrysler, announced a partnership to develop, within a decade, vehicles that would be three times more fuel-efficient than today's cars. The government has called this effort, involving more than $1 billion contributed jointly by all partners, "a technical challenge comparable to or greater than . . . the Apollo project" (Nauss, 1993).

Partnerships come in virtually all sizes, shapes, and classifications. They exist in both the private and public sectors, and, as we've discussed, sometimes bridge them. They can be between two people who share the same office. Or they can transcend industry and national borders. They can be composed of organizations ranging from the world's largest to its smallest. Or they can be combinations of organizations of all sizes. They can exist for an indefinite period of time. Or they can, if the partners wish, operate for a very limited time. They can exist for any number of reasons. And they can involve virtually anyone from business associates to friends, family members, or spouses.

Risky Business

We think it is important to note that while the basic partnership structure has been around since the beginning of time, contemporary partnerships are redefining some of its most basic elements. For starters, they perceive power relationships differently. Many of today's partnerships are responding to the erosion of hierarchy and patriarchy, attempting to distribute power differently. As Peter Block mentions in his book *Stewardship: Choosing Service over Self Interest* (1993), "If the issues of real power, control, and choice are not addressed and renegotiated, then our efforts to change organizations become an exercise in cosmetics" (p. 27).

To be competitive in today's and tomorrow's world, partnerships will need to be connected in another way, so that power between the people and the organizations involved is roughly balanced. Partnerships that move beyond form and structure—those that demand deeper changes, in principles and behavior—will recognize the interdependence of multiple parties and replace control with cooperation and collaboration. This shift in the balance of power both requires and creates a greater demand for equity in our interpersonal and institutional relationships. This reorientation is causing contemporary partnerships to blur their boundaries, expand their focus, and take a longer view that measures the quality of their services, to multiple users, at many different points through highly interdependent enterprises.

One irony we found in our exploration of partnerships is that, while they are increasingly popular, they remain quite risky. About one out of every three partnerships we studied, for example, either failed outright, could survive only in a radically restructured form after one or more of the initial partners dropped out, or survived only because the partners could not extricate themselves from unhappy or unrewarding situations. Other studies confirm that these findings are not unusual. One recent survey of forty-nine international partnerships for the *Harvard Business Review*, for example, discovered that one out of three were considered outright failures by both partners (Bleeke and Ernst, 1991). Other estimates run as high as one out of two.

Still an Irresistible Force

While partnerships can—and often do—take a toll on people and organizations, they continue to be born at ever increasing rates. Despite great risks, they have increasingly become an irresistible force in the workplace. IBM, for example—once the supreme example of vertical integration—has now invested capital in no fewer than two hundred important partner-suppliers in order to protect and enhance the ability of these companies to add value to IBM's products and services (Flagg, 1992). Rather than the exception, this example is rapidly becoming the rule.

As we watch all these new partnerships being born, the question becomes *why*. Why, at this time in our history, have people and organizations all around the world found partnerships so attractive—so attractive they'll turn away from familiar structures that have worked well (or at least satisfactorily) for years; so attractive they'll commit to expensive and often excruciating change processes; so attractive they'll "bet the farm," sometimes risking the future of an entire enterprise on an idea that, for them, is unproven?

The reasons vary, of course, according to whoever supplies them. But, in our research, we found that six reasons were given by partners time and time again. It's not coincidental that these reasons are all related to emerging trends in the work environment—trends that make the prospect of partnering all the more compelling.

1. *In an age of limited and diminishing resources, partnerships offer expanded capabilities, allowing organizations to do more with less or to do something entirely different than their existing resource base permits.* Increasingly, professional people have found hierarchical structures too inefficient to achieve their goals. Perhaps the most highly publicized result of this thinking has been the enormous number of lay-offs that have occurred in large companies around the world. These were more than a response to recession; they represent a fundamental restructuring of these organizations (both public and private). In order to survive, organizations have had to find ways to get more accomplished with fewer employees. As a result they are learning to share their capital, people, and time with unlikely entities. Vendors partner with suppliers, competitors with competitors, businesses with customers, for-profit organizations with nonprofit organizations.

At the same time we see many of their laid-off employees becoming independent contractors, vendors, consultants, and other kinds of partners (often for the very organizations that laid them off). The organizations not only have less overhead, but also more flexibility in adjusting their resources to meet demands. They can, for example, call people in only during heavy periods when they need extra help. Their new partners have both work opportunities at the organization and the freedom to develop additional customers elsewhere. Both the companies and their new partners can benefit.

2. *In an age of intense and turbulent change and shifting boundaries, partnerships enable companies to be more flexible, to leverage competencies and share resources, to create new ventures that would have been*

inconceivable on their own. Today, the pace and direction of change is often unpredictable and inconsistent. We often see rapid change existing beside stability and stagnation. Increasingly, realities such as these require new, more situationally based structures that are fundamentally incompatible with hierarchies. To survive in these turbulent times, organizations must be nimble, adaptable, and often subservient to some higher purpose. People and organizations must recognize their deep interdependence. This is the opposite of the self-reliance and independence that hierarchical structures value.

Unlike hierarchies, which are normally established with pyramid-like permanence in mind, partnerships can be either as permanent or as transient as the partners wish. Lacking the capacity to manufacture its entire line of PowerBook notebooks, for example, Apple Computer turned to Sony Corporation in 1991 to produce the least-expensive version. A year later, after selling more than one hundred thousand Sony-made models, Apple had gotten what it wanted from the partnership. So it simply ended the agreement (Byrne, Brandt, and Port, 1993).

Similarly, individual authors come together to form temporary partnerships in order to produce a book. The three of us, for instance, formed a temporary partnership in the preparation of this book. Comparable examples can be found in many artistic fields, from Broadway musicals to large, outdoor sculptures. A West Coast museum recently went into partnership with a very successful theme park in order to gain assistance in controlling the crowds it anticipated for a special exhibit. In none of these cases was a long-term arrangement either anticipated or desired. Partnerships allow for the formation of flexible and temporary working relationships.

This kind of flexibility is taken to the logical extreme in the "virtual" model. Here there is not even the pretense of permanence of any kind. Organizations come together at a finger snap to exploit a fleeting opportunity, perform the necessary tasks, and then disband. Perhaps some or all of these organizations will come together again to take advantage of other such opportunities. But none is bound to work with any other. And all are free to pursue anything else that comes their way.

For someone used to working in hierarchies, the lack of security and continuity can seem quite disturbing. But for many people it's a matter of mind-set. "Sure, it's nice having a paycheck every two weeks," one education consultant told us. "But when you really give things a close look, job security is a myth. My father worked for the same company for thirty-five years. But that was in the '40s, '50s, and '60s, when many people worked for the same companies for decades. Now, no one—not even a government worker—has a guaranteed deal. Anything can change at any time. And the trick, I think, is to focus on the benefits of continually finding yourself in new situations and with new people—the constant discovery, the confluence of new ideas, the vitality."

3. *In an age of growing complexity, partnerships offer easy and convenient access to specialized resources.* Today, the complexity of solutions can be mind-boggling. For example, a typical memory chip attached to a circuit board in a personal computer is made up of more than four million transistors and other minute components. Making the chip alone requires legions of manufacturing equipment vendors as well as chip designers, process technology engineers, and fabrication and assembly workers. To produce these kinds of products quickly and cost-effectively increasingly requires the kind and volume of specialized expertise that organizations—either large or small—just cannot afford to support in-house. So, once again, partnering becomes the obvious solution. And, once again, we're seeing this across the organizational spectrum.

On the one hand, for example, we find that many small businesses have an informal or even a formal partnership with a CPA firm, a payroll service, or a marketing agency that provides specialized services they can't afford or don't need on a full-time or even an extended part-time basis. Larger nonprofit organizations often avail themselves of such contracted services as well as a means of reducing costs. Furthermore, large nonprofits are increasingly moving into consortia with other nonprofit organizations in order to share medical, dental, and disability plans or to share administrative staff, professional development services, libraries, computers, or other expensive resources and technologies.

Members of a consortium of graduate schools in northern California are now coordinating and sharing information about their students' field placement experiences. Many of these same schools have formed a library consortium to facilitate interlibrary loans, and they hope to soon build a unified, computerized catalogue of books and periodicals, so that any student or faculty member can readily access information about holdings at any participating school. Similar arrangements are cropping up in schools and human service agencies throughout the United States. While these institutions often compete against one another for students or community funds, they have found that cooperation through formal partnerships is essential to their continuing survival, given the funding crises facing all human service and educational organizations today.

4. *In an age of growing globalization, partnerships can offer a wider geographic reach into diverse global markets, allowing for approaches that are customized for local markets and individual consumers.* Businesses are being forced to respond to a growing diversity of marketplace interests. We are living in an age of dual paradoxes: expanding territories and shifting boundaries on the one hand, and a growing need to affiliate and/or establish identities based on special interests on the other hand. For American businesses, in particular, this is a new challenge. In 1950, for example, the United States accounted for more than 40 percent of the world's entire gross national product. During the next couple of decades, many American companies continued to think that the U.S. market was the only really important market. But with the economic revitalization of Europe; the amazing rise of Japan, South Korea, Singapore, Taiwan, and other Pacific Rim nations; and now the startling eco-

nomic turnabouts in many Latin American nations, this thinking has changed dramatically.

Other national and regional markets are no longer afterthoughts, but prime targets for growth. Increasingly, resources are being committed to international arenas. And also increasingly, companies have realized that to enter foreign markets they will have to look outside their corporate walls. They will have to seek out people and organizations that can help them break into—and succeed in—these new markets. And, once again, the very nature of hierarchical organizations hampers such a process.

As we turn to worldwide efforts at partnership, we might also pause long enough to examine the partnerships that have been formed within other countries to foster international cooperation. Many businesses in Taiwan, for instance, were originally formed by young entrepreneurs who combined their limited resources to build a new company. As their companies matured, these visionary men and women found a new reason for their partnerships. They discovered that each partner brought a certain expertise to the business, regarding specific foreign nations with which they wanted to do business.

A company in Taiwan that produces frozen Chinese dinners has made full use of one partner's fluency in English and four years of college in the United States to open up the American market to their product; they have similarly made use of the experiences of a second partner to break into the European market. Many of these Taiwanese companies have also formed partnerships with large foreign corporations in order to compete effectively in the international arena. A small pharmaceutical company in Taiwan is now partnering with a large American drug company, while many Taiwanese car dealerships have established close working partnerships with major Japanese automakers.

The same type of arrangements are now being negotiated in Eastern Europe. Newly emerging entrepreneurs are forming partnerships with one another in order to pool financial resources and expertise. As in Taiwan, they are also beginning to form partnerships with foreign companies—ranging from McDonald's and Coca-Cola to much smaller tool-and-die, scrap metal, and toy manufacturing firms located in Western Europe or the United States.

There is also a growing reliance on partnering beyond the corporate world to achieve greater geographic reach and influence. In fact, entire nations are now partnering in ways many of us would have never thought possible several years ago. Perhaps the most dramatic example of this trend is the emerging reality of the European Community (EC), for decades a dream of visionary Europeans. The 1990s have become the EC's moment of truth, the decade in which it must deliver on the dream. Already, much of the dream has become a reality. On January 1, 1993, most of the restrictions that hampered travel, trade, and commerce among European countries were eliminated. And in the years to come, the EC may integrate in ways that have been unprecedented among nations, introducing such innovations as a common currency and passports.

While much attention has been focused on European unity, similar partnership arrangements among nations are very much in evidence throughout the world; they are likely to become even more evident with the establishment of new trade agreements among the major nations in the world market. In Eastern Europe and Central Asia, for example, former Soviet republics have created the Commonwealth of Independent States. In South America, Brazil, Argentina, Paraguay, and Uruguay—once closed, government-controlled economies all—have formed Mercosur, their own EC-style common market.

5. *Fifth, as technology gives rise to independent and often impersonal work, partnerships satisfy a human need for community; they formally recognize our deep interdependence on each other to get a job done.* In contrast to hierarchical organizations, partnerships typically concentrate on joining rather than differentiating. People come together as peers for mutual benefit. They look for shared interests, goals, and benefits—often reinforced by a shared sense of a higher

purpose. They recognize the need to take common risks, and they are pleased to receive common rewards. They are not partitioned into the leaders and the led. They are not separated into winners and losers. They are each a part of the whole, working together for an intrinsically better life.

Indeed, partnerships can have a humanizing, harmonizing, spiritually satisfying effect that is extremely difficult, if not impossible, to achieve within a hierarchical organization. As Chris, the philosophical disk jockey on TV's *Northern Exposure*, said at the end of one episode, when he gave up controlling interest in a local bar: "Happiness doesn't come from owning things. Happiness comes from being a part of things."

6. *In an age of growing egalitarianism, partnerships offer the chance for increased personal involvement, control, and professional fulfillment.* In the 1976 film *Network*, Peter Finch plays Howard Beale, a long-time network news anchorman who tells his audience of millions, "I'm mad as hell, and I'm not going to take this anymore." One of the reasons for this line's enduring popularity is how deeply it resonates with people throughout the world who work in hierarchical organizations. Increasingly, men and women have become frustrated with the hierarchical model, particularly if they are working in large organizations. Often they see themselves as being at the mercy of limited superiors, left out of the decision-making process, stifled creatively, hamstrung by bureaucratic regulations, and much more. In a growing number of cases, people are willing to work harder and to forfeit traditional job benefits in order to take greater control over their destiny.

There are a number of reasons for this growing dissatisfaction. One is the increasing lack of faith in the effectiveness of hierarchies to meet today's organizational needs. Another, quite interestingly, is the increasingly rights-oriented perspective of younger workers (Naisbitt, 1984). Raised to take democracy seriously and to place a higher value on individual rights, a growing number of workers entering the workplace in the 1970s and 1980s found the entire concept of hierarchy increasingly alien and unattractive. More and more, these people have wanted to be involved in making decisions rather than just in implementing them. More and more they have been drawn to various partnership-style arrangements that exist within or between large organizations. Or, alternatively, they turn to small businesses. While they are likely to find more comfortable workplaces, they are also exposed to the vulnerability and scarce resources of the small organization. Under such conditions, partnership once again becomes important (albeit to protect an organization's viability rather than to escape hierarchical restraints).

The Essential Points

1. Partnerships are often formed to yield *efficiency*. Partnerships allow participating organizations to do more with less. They provide high-quality products or services at lower costs than is possible working in isolation.

2. Partnerships provide *flexibility*. Their structures and agreements can readily be changed to meet shifting needs and conditions.

3. Partnerships offer expanded *resources*. Partners have easier, more convenient access to important specialized resources such as expertise, space, technology, and materials.

4. Partnerships often create *expanded markets* for their participating organizations, including a wider geographic reach and/or access to new segments of an established market.

5. Partnerships offer their participants a *sense of interdependence*. They offer both connections and community, increasing their participants' involvement with and reliance on people in other participating organizations.

6. Partnerships offer an increased opportunity for *personal gratification*, including increased personal involvement, control, and professional fulfillment.

Chapter Two

The Nature of Effective Partnership

In Chapter One we defined six major benefits partnerships provide in our turbulent and demanding postmodern era. The next step is to determine how best to design partnerships so that they effectively deliver these benefits. Drawing on previous studies and our own consultations, this chapter addresses how to take unique advantage of this particular form of collaboration.

We can begin by noting that partnerships—unlike other organizational forms—involve the formation of relationships between entities (individuals or organizations) that retain substantial independence. The complex system that is formed includes a nonhierarchical structure, a collaboration-based culture, and a relatively equitable distribution of power and authority among the partnership's chief participants. Partnerships also differ from many other organizational forms in that they are often formed in order to produce a specific product or service rather than to affect the overall operations of an organization or company.

When we examine these distinguishing characteristics more carefully we gain a clearer picture not only of what sets partnerships apart, but also what distinguishes successful from unsuccessful partnerships. In this chapter we will examine the nature of effective partnerships through seven lenses: (1) shared direction, (2) structure, (3) systems, (4) culture, (5) operations, (6) competency, and (7) leadership and management. (See Table 2.1)

Shared Direction

Traditional, autonomous organizations are, by definition, company-focused: for-profit organizations are successful to the extent that they

Table 2.1. A Comparison of Hierarchical Organizations and Partnerships.

	Hierarchical organizations	Partnerships

Shared direction
  Vision
  Mission
  Strategy
  Goals
  Objectives
  Tactics
	Company focus	Industry or market focus

Structure
  Communication flow
  Access to information:
    frequency, quality,
    perceived value
	Pyramidal	Flat or networked

Systems
  Management practices
  Information technology
  Continuous improvement
    and redesign
	Top down or bottom up	Interactive

Culture
  Values
  Beliefs
  Behaviors
	Paternalistic	Collaborative

Operations
  Research and development
  Production
  Marketing
  Servicing
  Financing
	Productive	Adaptive

Competency
  Role (job)
  Function or project
  Business
  Market
  Industry
	Function-driven	Process-driven

Leadership and management
  Human resources
  Financial resources
  Time
  Space
	Position-based	Initiative- or team-based

Source: Adapted from materials created by HMRG, Inc.

remain financially viable; nonprofit organizations are successful to the extent that they continue to be supported by the constituencies they serve. In fact, in many sectors of the business community a company is considered successful primarily if it is able to crowd out its competition and command a larger share of its market.

Partnerships, on the other hand, are by definition not company-focused. They frequently involve several different organizations which may (in other settings) actually compete against one another in a specific market. Partnerships are industry- or market-focused. The members of a partnership are primarily concerned with improving the quality of the product or service they provide, better serving their mutual customers, and finding ways in which they together can gain a greater share in their mutual market or broaden the scope of the market for which they sometimes compete. In other words, partnerships concentrate on expanding the size of the pie rather than on competing for the biggest piece of the existing pie.

Typically, a partnership is based on a specific product or service that all members of the partnership share in common, or on a specific customer base that all partners serve. As we look at the different kinds of missions that partnerships embrace, we will turn first to product- or service-based partnerships and then to customer-based partnerships.

Product- and Service-Based Partnerships

Typically, a product- or service-based partnership is organized to accomplish one or more of three goals. First, it may link together stages or steps in production or in the provision of services, thereby reducing costs and/or improving quality. In her study of partnerships, Kanter (1994) concludes that these "value-chain" partnerships are among the strongest and most closely bound of any she studied. Many companies that were previously isolated as autonomous vendors and purchasers are now linking together through partnership in ways that give both organizations greater control over both cost and quality. And, rather than working with multiple vendors, some organizations are now establishing single-vendor relationships that are particularly valuable when a new, specialized product or service is needed.

USAir, for example, formed a partnership with AT&T to develop an integrated voice-data network that connects its airline reservation centers to its data communications network (Jewett, 1991). This vendor-purchaser partnership saved USAir approximately $500,000 in 1991. Similarly, Puma (a sporting goods company) established a partnership with GE to build a computer system to manage its sales force. We will focus on another vendor-purchaser partnerships (Lesher Communications–Norpac) as one of three case studies in Part Three.

The second goal that is frequently at the heart of a product-or service-based partnership is to expand into a new product or service line. Partnerships of this type can reduce risks and often costs as well. Kanter (1994) characterizes this type of partnership arrangement, a "joint venture," as one that requires moderate strength and closeness. Joint ventures have been of enormous value to many small- to medium-sized companies, including TelePad Corporation of Reston, Virginia. With the help of more than two dozen strategic partners and suppliers, TelePad has been able to draw upon the specialized resources it needs to develop its new pen-based computer, a product the company could never have brought to market on its own (Byrne, Brandt, and Port, 1993).

The third goal many product- or service-based partnerships seek to fulfill concerns combining resources for the production of a single product or service. Kanter (1994) describes these "mutual service" partnerships as being among the weakest of any type she studied. By combining resources (including capital, facilities, staff, expertise, and knowledge), members of a partnership can often reduce costs and improve quality, or even accomplish something that would not otherwise be possible.

Classic examples of this kind of partnership are the temporary alliances formed between government agencies, industry, and community groups throughout the United States to address complex and often controversial environmental problems. In Idaho, for instance, the Coeur d'Alene Mines Corporation wanted to engage in long-term reclamation and environmental management of areas it had once extensively mined. Lacking reclamation expertise, the mining company contacted the Wildlife Habitat Enhancement Council (WHEC) in Silver Spring, Maryland, which helped the company not only develop an overall plan but also recruit college students as interns. Martin (1994) offers this and many other examples of companies, consulting firms, colleges and universities, human service agencies, and government agencies in the Pacific Northwest working on environmental problems through partnerships.

Equally impressive partnerships have been established between autonomous arts institutions in many cities in the United States to feature unified themes for a specific period of time. In Denver, for instance, the city's public library, art galleries, symphony orchestra, and museums collaborated during the 1970s to offer special programs on specific historical periods and other themes. Other cities have similarly coordinated efforts between artistic organizations to plan special celebrations and joint commemorations of distinctive moments in the city's history or even for mutual solicitation of private funds.

Customer-Based Partnerships

With the increasing emphasis in recent years on the customer's role in defining quality, there has been a corresponding rise in the formation of customer-oriented partnerships. If it takes little additional time or money for an organization (through partnership) to make its customers happier and more likely to use its products or services in the future or to support its continued funding (for nonprofits), then traditional organizational boundaries are likely to continue to be broken.

In many instances these customer-based partnerships are established to link products or services that are offered to a single customer by disparate organizations, thereby reducing costs for the participating organizations while improving product or service quality. Small, independent food stores, for example, sometimes form partnerships to establish a single marketplace (in the old farmers' market tradition). Five or six take-out restaurants in a shopping mall might similarly form a partnership to lease, design, and manage a common eating area. They might also jointly hire entertainers, coordinate seasonal decoration, or share advertising space and costs.

These types of partnerships are also established to help organizations expand into new customer populations, thereby increasing revenues and reducing risks. As noted in Chapter One, this has become particularly prevalent in recent years due to the movement of American businesses into foreign markets. While many American corporations are looking beyond nation-state boundaries for new customers, others are making use of partnerships to find new customers and markets at home. In some cases—such as the partnership between Arthur Andersen and the Alameda Unified School District that we will be studying extensively in Part Three—an organization that wants to expand its market base forms a partnership with representatives of that very market. Community colleges in western Canada, for instance, will often establish a partnership with a trade union when moving into a new vocational field that is represented by that union. Similarly, many innovative corporations are now establishing potential-user groups to advise them on ways in which to market a new product. These new marketing partnerships embrace an important marketing principle that the social psychologist Kurt Lewin taught us many years ago: the best way to gain a person's acceptance for a new product is to ask their advice about how best to market the product (Marrow, 1969).

A third focus of customer-based partnerships is for bringing multiple customers together, thereby increasing revenues and reducing costs. An early form of this type of facilitated resource-sharing were temporary secretarial and accounting services. More recently some financial institutions, such as the Bank of America, have made their own internal payroll service available to various small businesses, thereby sharing their own overhead costs, generating revenues, and providing yet another distinctive service to small businesses that enhances their competitive advantage. Furthermore, we find that many small businesses are in informal or even formal partnerships with CPA firms, accounting services, or marketing agencies that provide specialized services that these businesses could not themselves afford or do not need on a full-time basis. In addition, large nonprofits are increasingly moving into partnership arrangements with other nonprofit organizations to share medical, dental, and disability plans; administrative or professional development services; and libraries, computers, or other expensive resources and technologies.

These modest partnerships have set the stage for more ambitious resource-sharing partnerships—often called "consortia"—that embrace an even greater commitment to institutional interdependence. Many liberal arts colleges in the United States have established consortia that enable them to offer joint courses (thus reducing instructional costs), build single library collections (often mediated through intercampus loan agreements and electronic cataloguing), and venture together into new program areas.

Corporations have similarly formed consortia to share many different corporate resources, ranging from secretarial, copying, janitorial, and messenger services to certain manufacturing functions. Partnership arrangements of this type have been established between IBM and the Solectron Corporation, Eastman Kodak and IBM, and Businessland and Digital Equipment Corporation (Stuckey, 1993). (We will focus on one such consortium in Part Three—the Council for Continuous Improvement, created for the sharing of expertise and information.) Such support services are becoming increasingly expensive for individual businesses. Moreover, equipment that might supplant these support services is likewise becoming increasingly complex and expensive, and the data that businesses use are becoming increasingly centralized in massive data banks. Thus we are likely to find increasing use of partnerships that bring together and coordinate services and information. Those organizations that move readily into these kind of relationships are likely to thrive in today's turbulent, demanding environment. And those people and organizations that specialize in the formation of these partnerships will find themselves in great demand in our changing world.

Structure

Organizations in the United States have typically been hierarchical, not only because this was the structure most of us were comfortable with, but also because there frankly has been very little pressure to change. Most American corporations, human service agencies, and government offices could successfully operate within a hierarchical structure providing those in charge were skilled in interpersonal relationships, knowledgeable about the organization's operations, and committed to long hours of work. In some cases, however, the hierarchical structure was still an impediment. As a result, one of three kinds of partnership have been formed.

Partnerships of Agreement

Because of legal constraints or precedence in a particular field, what we call "partnerships of agreement" have been formed among certain organizations. The legal entities that are commonly formed between lawyers and physicians typifies this type of partnership. This type of partnership exists primarily in form, not function. Typically, partnerships of agreement are intended to preserve traditional ways of operating a business. They usually are motivated primarily by legal compliance.

Formal agreements lie at the heart of these enterprises. Professional partnerships involving lawyers, accountants, physicians, architects, and psychologists are usually based on complex, formal contracts and often include some sharing of administrative resources (secretarial, accounting, and so forth) as well as leases, equipment, or library resources. These partnerships of agreement are likely to remain active in the near future, but they are clearly not a growth area, given the acquisition of many of these partnerships in recent years by much larger companies and the movement in many of these professions to a more business-oriented or corporate mentality.

Partnerships of Function

Another partnership structure—what we call "partnerships of function"—has emerged more recently. This type of partnership is established when it makes sense for two organizations to work closely together for the sort of pragmatic reasons we identified in Chapter One, or because they share interests such as those we identified above with regard to shared direction. A majority of the partnerships formed today are partnerships of function. Function-oriented partnerships are characterized not by compliance and legal agreements, but rather by complementarity, compensatory relationships, and expansion.

One of the most popular arrangements, particularly among companies where research and development plays a large role, is the "cross-licensing agreement." This kind of arrangement enables companies to share specific information or expertise for mutual benefit. In the pharmaceutical industry, for example, Merck, Eli Lilly, Fujisawa, and Bayer aggressively cross-license their newest drugs to one another, not only to support industrywide innovation, but also to apportion the high fixed costs of R&D and distribution (Lei and Slocum, 1991).

Another very popular form of function-oriented partnership is the "strategic alliance." This too is a formal pact between two or more organizations to achieve a mutual goal or set of goals. It is distinguished from a cross-licensing arrangement in at least two important ways. First, the sharing can involve any number of assets, from product expertise to knowledge of specific markets. Second, the degree of sharing is often much greater. For example, Corning Incorporated has two dozen joint ventures, with such foreign partners as

Siemens of Germany, Samsung of Korea, Asahi Chemical of Japan and CIBA-GEIGY of Switzerland, both to enter a growing number of related high-technology markets and to succeed in them (Lei and Slocum, 1991).

Joint-powers agreements, a species of strategic alliance, have become popular with public agencies. Independent government agencies that share a common purpose, are faced with a similar problem, or have overlapping or adjacent jurisdictions form an alliance to accomplish specific goals (such as redevelopment of a specific urban area), solve common problems (such as cleaning up an adjoining river) or coordinate interagency activities (such as collaboration between two agencies that assist the same foreign governments).

Increasing privatization of public services is spawning a growing number of these joint powers agreements (Drucker, 1989). Local, regional, and state governments are sharing their resources and experience to improve the efficiency and effectiveness of their services in an effort to compete for survival. We have also seen the birth of a whole new set of agreements between regions on a global level—the EC, OPEC, NAFTA, and so on—as the world rearranges its economic power base.

Partnerships of Commitment

A third structure, identified as "partnerships of commitment," is less common today, but may become more common in the future, as an increasing number of organizations come to recognize the inherent value of extensive partnership-based cooperation and collaboration. This structure is characterized by collaboration and joint development. Many different arrangements have recently been explored to make this extensive sharing of resources, relationships, and values possible.

Two such structures have received considerable attention in recent years: the "hollow corporation" and the "virtual corporation." In many respects both are extensions of the strategic alliance. They dramatically reshape the way organizations develop and deliver their products and services. They both imply real-time, interactive, highly adaptive responses to an ever-changing environment. These two partnership models represent a dramatic rejection of the hierarchical, vertically integrated, stable corporations that have long dominated many industries. In the large, traditional corporation that was vertically integrated, virtually all the elements that went into the finished products, from circuit boards to spark plugs, were developed and manufactured in-house for eventual use in another product made by another part of the organization. The aim was to provide cost-efficiency and quality assurance by controlling the development, manufacturing, and marketing processes. In its heyday, a company like IBM was the ideal example of this type of organization. Not only did it make and market computers, it also made the circuit boards that went into the computers, the microchips that went onto the circuit boards, and, in many cases, the equipment necessary to manufacture the microchips.

In many respects the hollow corporation and the virtual corporation represent near opposites of this vertical-integrative process. In a hollow corporation, many, if not all, components of a product are made outside the company. Cirrus Logic, a microchip supplier in San Jose, California, is a good example. It often receives orders for very specialized logic chips, and custom designs the chips to fit customer specifications. Then it sends the designs to an external facility that fabricates, tests, and assembles them and even stamps Cirrus's logo on them. After the chips are delivered to Cirrus, the company sends them to the customer. The benefits of this arrangement, especially for a small company such as Cirrus, are much greater flexibility and lower overhead. Cirrus can do the job for less because it does not have to do the job all by itself.

A virtual corporation is a somewhat different concept. Essentially it is a network of companies that can quickly be brought together to seize fast-changing and often short-lived opportunities.

Instead of growing as its business grew, for example, Kingston Technology, a personal computer upgrader based in Fountain Valley, California, created a rock-solid network of partners and farmed work out to them. This, as the company is quick to point out, is not mere subcontracting or "outsourcing." Kingston and its partners lead complementary corporate lives, sharing capital, know-how, and markets. Because each specializes in what it does, Kingston has been able to cut loose from the costs of running a larger-scale enterprise and cash in on efficiencies that often elude its rivals. Kingston's president, John Tu, also claims that the company saves enormous amounts on lawyers' fees, because it doesn't base its agreements on formal contracts. "We do almost all our business on a handshake," he says with pride (Meyer, 1993).

Systems

In traditional organizations, information typically flows from the top to the bottom. Authority is also typically set at the top of the organization, and primary leadership roles are played by those who manage people working under them and control various operations. System theorists speak of the critical role played by the "leading part" in a system—that component of any traditional system that monitors, controls, and integrates other disparate and often highly specialized components of the system. When it comes to partnerships, these traditional functions are called into question as both unnecessary and inappropriate.

First, in a partnership information tends to flow from side to side rather than from top to bottom. Interactive networks typify successful partnerships. The Boeing Aircraft Company, for instance, had traditionally designed its new aircraft and then marketed them to potential customers. Now, through partnership agreements, Boeing brings in the customer (such as United Airlines) to help it design the new aircraft right from the start (Weiner, 1990). General Electric similarly brought in one of its customers (and sometime competitor), Sears, to help it design new appliances (Jick, 1990).

In partnerships, authority tends to be distributed evenly or in a changing (and sometimes even ambiguous) manner among the partners. There is rarely a static authority structure in an active partnership. Furthermore, there is either no "leading part" in the partnership, or there are multiple leading parts and the partnership itself provides the primary guiding, leadership function.

As Kanter (1994) concluded, successful partnerships "cannot be controlled by normal systems but require a dense web of interpersonal connections and internal infrastructures that enhance learning" (p. 97). This dense web, in turn, requires frequent and clear communication, a respect for differences, and flexibility— ingredients that have repeatedly shown up in our own analyses of successful partnerships.

Because there are fluid lines and bases of authority, partners can't rely on written agreements or memoranda when communicating with one another. Authority shifts in subtle ways that often require at least brief in-person interactions among the partners. Furthermore, if there are more than two partners, these interactions usually must take place with all partners in the room at the same time, for shifts in power and authority are often even more subtle and surprisingly rapid in a dynamic, multiple-member partnership. Successful partnerships clearly require moving beyond the safety net of legal contracts (the partnerships of agreement described above) to a shifting, dynamic relationship based on trust and communication (partnerships of commitment).

Culture

Many contemporary gurus of American business write of the new business "paradigm" (see Ray and Rinzler, 1993). We suggest that this new paradigm relates specifically to an emphasis on collaboration and flexibility—factors that seem to be prominent in any successful partnership. This paradigm shift from competition and the struggle for power to cooperation and the establishment of trust parallels the shift in social values from "the blade" to "the chalice" that

Eisler (1987) describes in her thoughtful and provocative reexamination of Western history. For Eisler, social structures are most successful if they serve as chalices—as containers—to bring about community and mutual caring, rather than as weapons (blades) for domination.

Psychologists often tell us that anxiety is reduced when it can be bounded and contained by a supportive structure or environment (see Colman and Bexton, 1975). The chalice serves as a container for the anxiety that inevitably occurs in society. A turbulent and unpredictable society such as we live in today is likely to be filled with anxiety, and in such a society boundaries are at best ambiguous if not nonexistent (Jameson, 1991). In such a society one typically tries to reduce anxiety through control and domination (the blade)—that is, by asserting and ensuring one's own individual rights. Eisler and other social theorists (such as Gilligan, 1982, and Bellah and others, 1985, 1991) suggest an alternative approach that emphasizes the formation of community and an ethic of mutual caring—one in which individual rights are balanced off against collective responsibility.

Certainly in the case of partnerships there are ambiguous boundaries and often turbulence and unpredictability. The conditions are ripe for debilitating anxiety and a resulting attempt to reassert control and domination. However, if the anxiety can be bounded and contained, then partners will be willing to take risks and to dream—both of which are essential to partnerships.

One of the critical roles of leaders in any institution is to create a culture within their own organization that is supportive and safe. While it is clear that most of our organizations dwell in highly competitive environments and are in need of the blade, it is also clear that the culture within these organizations must serve not only (or even primarily) as the blade, encouraging competition and domination, but also (or alternatively) as a chalice, a container for organization anxiety.

In their discussions regarding a new paradigm for business,

members of the World Business Academy recently focused on this interplay between competition and cooperation (Joba, Maynard, and Ray, 1993). They noted that at its best competition can serve as a motivator for individuals and companies to strive toward higher-quality performance. Furthermore, the friction that exists in competition can "spark a fire," serving as a catalyst for higher achievement. Yet, competition can also be destructive, creating rather than ameliorating organizational anxiety. These discussants noted that cooperation is more likely than competition to bring out the best in us, though it can too often focus on processes and relationships without being productive. They suggested that a third mode—co-creation—combines the best of competition and cooperation with an effective balance between goal and process orientation. In co-creation, the boundaries are open between the participants as they share responsibility for creating a new product or service.

In creating a culture that promotes cooperation and perhaps even co-creation, we must beat at least some of our institutional swords (for example, competition for career advancement and rewards based on individual rather than group achievements) into plowshares. We must begin to encourage and acknowledge not only the competitive edge but also the cooperative agreement. We must begin to reward group success; we must find room in our organizations for what the bumper stickers are now calling "random acts of kindness."

This shift to a "plowshare" or a blended sword-plowshare paradigm of business typically calls for a shift in the basic values, beliefs, and patterns of leadership in an organization—in other words, a change in the organizational culture. In such an organizational culture—and, in particular, in a function-oriented partnership or a partnership of commitment—we are encouraged to move from confrontation and competition to acceptance and collaboration. We are inspired to develop and sustain a respect for not only individual rights but also for collective responsibility as we move from competition to cooperation. If we want to move beyond cooperation to co-creation—if we want to shift from a function-oriented partnership to a partnership of commitment—then we are challenged to create an organizational culture and community of shared commitment and interdependency in the midst of alienation and rampant individualism. In such an organization we look for commonality in a world of competing interests.

James Houghton, the president of Corning, describes just such a commitment to the "plowshare" paradigm when he describes his own company (Nanda and Bartlett, 1991) as an "evolving network of wholly owned business and joint ventures" (p. 457). His sense of partnership within his own organization, as well as in joint ventures with many other companies worldwide, constitutes the basic culture in Corning. Houghton goes on to describe this culture and his notion of Corning as a network organization: "A network is egalitarian. The parent company does not dominate its offspring units. All operations are part of a family, some more distant cousins than others, but all possessing some shared ethics and values. In fact, I now describe joint venture partnerships as part of our strategic wheel. We take technology from the hub and spread it across each sector of our network—to the inner wheel of our divisions and subsidiaries, and to the outer wheel of our alliances" (p. 457).

In establishing this "network organization," Houghton made the key contacts with other organizations he wanted to form a partnership with (for example, Dow Chemical); however, he soon left the ongoing leadership to those people who would be responsible for the operations of the joint venture. While Houghton would initially join the board of a company he had just begun a major joint venture with, he would soon delegate this responsibility to one of his group presidents, thereby getting them more fully involved in and supportive of not only the partnership but also the concept of a network organization: "To make our network come alive, people at several levels have to move across borders. . . . Both joint venture partners have to recognize that moving bright, energetic people in and out of the alliances is not only acceptable—it is vital" (Nanda and Bartlett, 1991, p. 458).

A critical factor in the success of Corning (and probably most other large companies that have made effective use of partnerships) is not that the company is specifically out looking for partnerships to begin or join. Rather, Corning is successful at partnering because the basic culture of the organization encourages cooperation, the reduction or elimination of hierarchical, authoritarian relationships, and, in particular, the creation of a supportive, anxiety-reducing environment (Eisler's chalice). Effective partnerships with other organizations can't help but seed and blossom in such fertile soil.

Houghton points out that "our specific objective is not to create joint ventures, but to select a business structure that will provide the best chance of success in a particular market" (Nanda and Bartlett, 1991, p. 457). For a company such as Corning that seeks to create a collaborative, "plowshare" culture, joint ventures come more naturally and have a greater chance of survival than they do in companies with an organizational culture oriented toward competition and the blade. As Houghton puts it, "Something in our culture helps. We have grown up in this company with the Dow Corning success, where a handshake sealed an agreement and led to a remarkable partnership. We know these things can be successful. Besides, there has been a continuity in our relations with our partners at the chairman level. I make a point of getting together with the top person from each of our major partners once or twice a year, just to have lunch, if need be, and look the person in the eye to make sure our strategic visions match" (Nanda and Bartlett, 1991, p. 457).

In this statement Houghton identifies several of the keys to success in forming any partnership. First, he speaks of a tradition of successful partnerships. As we will demonstrate throughout this book, successful partnerships breed more successful partnerships. This success becomes embedded in the culture of an organization—in stories told about joint ventures and lessons repeatedly taught through anecdotes, jokes, and folk wisdom about "how we do business."

Second, a positive culture is strengthened through informal gestures, such as the handshake Houghton speaks of. A handshake implies a firm commitment and engenders a sense of trust in an organization's culture. This is critical to sustaining any supportive, plowshare culture. Third, Houghton speaks of continuity in leadership and frequent communication between those who head the organizations in a partnership. This continuity and integration—as we shall more fully discuss later in this chapter—seems to be critical to successful partnerships. Partnerships are simply too fragile and relationship-dependent for participating companies to be constantly shifting leaders or for their leaders not to be in frequent, face-to-face contact with one another. In sum, it seems that supportive cultures and successful partnerships both require exceptional leadership skills (see Schein, 1985).

Operations

Successful partnerships require extensive and skillful interaction among the parties involved. Given that partnerships require the crossing of traditional institutional boundaries, communication between participants is particularly likely to be distorted and intentions are particularly likely to be misunderstood. In Mamis's (1994) study of numerous partnerships, conducted for *Inc.* magazine, he found that there are inevitable conflicts among partners. He offered six "true confessions" that speak to the failure of partners to communicate:

1. "While I was out there working, they were in there plotting."
2. "My partners were fabulous as friends; as partners they were revolting."
3. "I made all the decisions; they made all the complaints."

4. "I spent the time; my partner spent the dough."

5. "My partner was a self-helper—to what was really mine."

6. "What, me worry?"

As we look more carefully at the stories underlying each of these statements, several communication themes become quite clear.

First, partnerships add stress to existing relationships, for they invariably bring up issues of control and authority. Partners must learn how to clearly and constructively talk about their relationships with regard to control and authority, for these issues are never permanently resolved in a dynamic partnership. Many of Mamis's stories involve misunderstandings regarding decision-making and budgetary authority in partnerships.

Second, the partners in Mamis's study got into trouble when they didn't keep each other informed about what they were doing. Frequent updates about partnership activities are essential; otherwise one or more partners will begin to imagine what the others are doing and may be particularly inclined to think the worst of their partners, especially if the issues of authority and control are also not discussed. Furthermore, ongoing communication must occur at all levels of the partnership, not just among its formal leaders or just among those involved in its day-to-day operations. Everyone must be kept informed. Often busy executives will communicate through nothing more than a monthly memorandum or a brief weekly phone call. Given this narrow window of opportunity, it is essential that communication occurs in a concise and convincing manner.

Third, it is very tempting, when faced with the complexity inherent in many partnerships, to remain ignorant of the regular details and problems of the organization. One can always assume (or at least hope) that problems will be taken care of by someone else (other partners or employees who are actually running the enterprise). We have often found in consulting with partnerships that no one is in charge. Each partner assumes that the other participating organizations have taken care of particular operations or specific problems. This abdication of responsibility ("What, me worry?") is often an even more serious problem than conflict over authority and control. It is very tempting for a busy business leader to forget for a while about that visionary (but marginal) partnership he or she set up six months ago.

Mamis's study suggests that partners must never abdicate responsibility; rather, the leaders of these companies must commit themselves from the start to regular communication about operations and problems, and they must dedicate their own time and/or the time of other key administrators to clear decision-making processes and collaborative problem-solving with the other partners. Thus partners not only need to have communication skills, they must also have a commitment to using these skills in a consistent manner.

Perhaps even more important than the quantity and timing of communication among partnership members is the skill required to make decisions and solve problems in a collaborative manner. Given that many partnership leaders are accustomed to giving orders or at least to managing within a clearly defined, hierarchical structure, the partnership offers a new challenge. Senge (1990) speaks of the value of dialogue, as opposed to just discussion, in contemporary organizations. When we communicate through dialogue, we seek out common understandings and shared values and visions, rather than trying to win over the other party or make our point (as we do in a discussion). Partnerships in particular need more dialogue and less discussion.

Competency

Partnerships typically require new structures, new systems, new operations, and even new cultures. Each of these changes, in turn, necessitates the acquisition of new competencies by those who participate in the partnerships. We suggest that three competencies are critical to successful partnerships. These competencies center on learning, as well as on the capacity to think critically and to clarify one's own personal aspirations as well as the organization's values. We will briefly touch on each of these competency areas, for they hold major implications for any company that is considering the formation of a major partnership.

Learning

Any partnership will inevitably involve learning for all parties involved. Even a company such as Corning, which has formed many partnerships, will learn from every new joint venture; for, if nothing else, the principal players in each new venture will learn about a new product, a different way of doing business, a different organizational culture, or (in the case of an international partnership) a different society.

Kanter (1994) focuses considerable attention on this element of learning in her study of successful partnerships: "Productive relationships usually require and often stimulate changes within the partners, changes that they may not anticipate at the outset of the collaboration. When two companies place themselves in intimate contact with each other through an alliance, it is almost inevitable that each will compare itself with the other: How do we measure up to our partner in systems sophistication or operational efficiency? What lessons can we learn from our partner? In fact, learning and borrowing ideas from partners is part of realizing the full value of the relationship" (p. 107).

Inevitably, new learning experiences will include the uncomfortable experience of making mistakes. In our own consulting experience we have rarely found mistake-free ventures. It is, in fact, not important that partners avoid making mistakes. It is only important that partners learn from their mistakes and don't continue to make the same mistake (Argyris and Schön, 1978). The first time an American business leader misinterprets the laughter of a Chinese businessman as a sign of overconfidence, or even indifference, she can be excused; however, if she is to be successful in this international venture she must soon learn that this laughter may actually be a sign of embarrassment or resistance. She can only come to this realization by actively reflecting on her own interactions with the Chinese businessman and by asking for feedback on her performance by colleagues who are more knowledgeable of Chinese culture. These two factors—critical reflection on one's own performance and solicitation of feedback—are central to active learning in any organizational setting (see Schön, 1983; Argyris and Schön, 1978; Senge, 1990) and are particularly important in complex partnerships.

Critical Thinking

When we enter into a partnership, we must begin not only to learn about the operations and culture of the other participants in the partnership, but must also at some level come to appreciate and even anticipate the implications of the perspectives held by members of these other companies. We must, in other words, begin to think like they think, even if we ourselves want to plan, manage, or solve problems in a somewhat different manner. This, in turn, requires that we reason and analyze from a relativistic frame of reference (Perry, 1970). We must be able to take several different perspectives into account, while also being clear about (and critical of) our own perspectives.

In deciding whether or not to enter into a partnership—and in selecting people to participate in its management—it is important to focus on critical thinking. Most people are not taught how to think critically; rather, it usually comes from considerable experience, from working in many different organizational settings, from experience with several different cultures and societies, and often from living through personal adversity. Thus, in looking for leadership among those starting a new partnership, age and diversity of experience may be just as important as technical expertise or problem-solving experience in an organization.

A second aspect of critical thinking is also particularly important in a partnership. Senge (1990) suggests that one must think systemically about one's own organization in our newly emerging postmodern world. Therefore, in the case of a partnership one must think systemically not only about one's own organization, but also about the partnership and all the other companies participating in it. The famous family therapist Virginia Satir (1972) often commented on the complexity of family systems, noting that as soon as you add a third or fourth element (for example, a first or second child) to the family equation, the level of complexity of the family—its dyadic, triadic, and quadratic relationships—begins to expand exponentially. Similarly, the complexity of a partnership increases exponentially with the addition of each partner to the organizational equation. The capacity to think systemically is critical for sheer survival in such a complex (and frequently changing) organizational setting. Once again, these skills are not easily taught; therefore, they must be taken into consideration in deciding whether or not to start or enter a partnership, in selecting those who will actively participate in it, and in deciding how many companies to invite into the partnership.

Clarification of Values

With unclear boundaries—both personal and organizational—it is particularly important that those participating in a partnership be clear about their mission and, in particular, about their own personal aspirations and the institutional values of the organizations involved. It is quite tempting to set up partnerships on a short-term basis for expediency's sake. But these partnerships often backfire.

Participants in a partnership must be clear about the reasons for setting up the partnership; this is why we devote so much time in this book to the issues of purpose, motivation, and values. We must at least be clear about values, purpose, and mission—for this clarity helps to contain the organizational anxiety that is inevitably generated by boundary-defying partnerships. If we indiscriminately set up partnerships, we are likely to lose any sense of our own personal identity and integrity. We are likely to be whipsawed from one promising venture to the next, and lose our sense of personal purpose and value while "fitting in" with the diverse cultures of many other partnering organizations. We end up losing our organizational "soul" while pursuing the potential benefits of partnership with other companies that offer many tempting resources and strategic advantages.

How do we gain the skills to clarify personal aspirations and institutional values? Unlike critical thinking, the competencies associated with clarification of aspirations and values can be learned. Typically all that is needed is time and someone who is skilled in helping people reflect on their own personal needs and dreams, as well as the needs and dreams of the organization they are part of and the partnership they have just formed (or are about to form or reexamine). Through reflection and dialogue, members of a partnership can make full use of all the learning and communication skills they have acquired in preparation for, or while working with, the partnership.

Leadership and Management

The primary role of leaders in a traditional, hierarchical organization is to monitor and control the ongoing operations of the organization; these are the typical traditional managerial functions. By contrast, the leadership role in a partnership is that of integrator of the partnership's functions and operations. Kanter (1994, pp. 103–104) provides us with some valuable insights regarding partnerships that we can apply to our understanding of leadership roles. She identifies five integrative functions that must operate in any successful partnership: strategic, tactical, operational, interpersonal, and cultural. We believe that each of these integrative functions requires effective leadership in any partnership.

The strategic integrative function is served when the various leaders of companies participating in a partnership keep in touch with one another. This way they not only share information about their individual companies, they also solve their mutual problems within the partnership. Kanter notes, for instance, that the chief executives of the European Retail Alliance devote one day each month to meeting together.

The leadership function that addresses the need for tactical integration is provided, typically, not by those at the top of the participating companies, but rather by mid-level managers who develop plans for specific projects or joint activities of the partnership. These mid-managers may even suggest changes in the structures of their own organizations—or the partnership—to ensure that the cooperative efforts of each company are being employed in an effective and efficient manner. When leadership is only provided at the top of participating companies, then (as we have found in our own consulting experiences), the partnership is likely to be nothing more than a novelty or "pet project" of the CEOs. The partnership is never faithfully or enthusiastically embraced or carried out by others in the participating companies.

A third leadership function in partnerships addresses the need for operational integration. This involves the provision of adequate resources (information, time, expertise) so that people doing the partnership projects and activities can actually carry out the day-to-day work. This type of leadership is provided by members of the training and organization development staff in many companies. Jick (1990) notes, for instance, that human resource (HR) development professionals often can play an invaluable role in helping to make a partnership successful: "All too often [partnership] relationships are mismanaged and synergies are underidentified or underutilized. . . . HR, however, can play a unique role in working with line management to improve the success rate of these partnership opportunities. Using many of the techniques and processes previously directed at intraorganizational change, HR professionals have an opportunity to facilitate and even accelerate these interorganizational relationships" (p. 436).

Interpersonal integration is provided by leaders at all levels of an organization. The formal leaders should bring together people from different levels of the participating organizations to get to know each other on a personal basis (much as the formal leaders typically got to know each other when forming the partnerships). Leadership in these informal gatherings is ultimately exhibited in spontaneous and often unpredictable ways by many different members of the participating companies. Expressions of concern for the welfare of employees from other partner organizations; genuine curiosity about the ways things are done in a partner company; a tangible expression of interest in learning from the new partnership enterprise—these are all forms of interpersonal leadership that make a partnership venture successful for everyone. The formal leadership of the participating companies can help set the tone for these interactions by establishing the culture and appropriate structures and systems for the partnership. The rest is inevitably up to the individual employees.

Finally, we suggest, along with Kanter, that effective leaders of partnerships typically provide cultural integration. Those who actually administer the partnership play a central role, according to Kanter, in creating this form of integration. Those who are actually managing the partnership must share some basic common values, as well as be open to the differences in values that exist among the participating companies. This is particularly important if the partnership involves men and women from different countries, ethnic groups, socioeconomic levels, or even geographic locations in the same country. Kanter notes that simple efforts to learn a few words in the dominant language of a partner company, or the participation of leaders from one of the partner companies in an orientation or training program offered by another partner company for its own employees, can make a big difference in terms of the success of a partnership.

Kanter speaks of the central risk in partnerships that is at the heart of each of these five integrative functions: the risk of change. We believe that leadership is central to each of these five integrative functions, for there is not likely to be much real action when an organization is faced with profound change unless leadership is manifest at all levels of the organization. We have consulted to many organizations and have ourselves participated (painfully) in many organizations that were poised on the brink of change, in response to shifting conditions within and surrounding the organization. Yet this change never occurred, in large part because there was neither the courage nor the commitment of leaders in the organization (at all levels) to the necessity of change or to the learning that inevitably accompanies any change process.

Fortunately or unfortunately, partnerships inevitably involve change; for when we enter such a relationship we open ourselves to alternative perspectives and needs, which we must somehow integrate with the dominant perspectives and needs within our own organization. We should not enter into any partnership if we are unwilling to be influenced by our partners. Furthermore, we should not enter into a partnership if we have not identified and nurtured courageous and committed leadership at all levels of our own organization.

The Essential Points

1. Because partnerships are without clear boundaries and are product-, service-, or customer-focused (rather than company-focused), they must have a clear, shared sense of direction.

2. Partnerships can be based on superficial legal agreements or on shared functional needs. Alternatively, they can become "partnerships of commitment," which take many different forms, ranging from strategic alliances to virtual corporations.

3. Partnerships, by necessity, require systems that are egalitarian and information-dependent.

4. An organizational culture of support and mutual care is needed to contain the organizational anxiety inevitably associated with boundary-defying partnerships.

5. Frequent and effective communication is more important in partnerships than in traditional, hierarchical organizations.

6. Partnerships require a commitment to learning, critical thinking, and clarity of personal aspirations and organizational values, and the associated competencies in these areas.

7. Leadership must be exhibited at all levels of companies participating in partnerships to provide strategic, tactical, operational, interpersonal, and cultural integration.

Part Two

How Partnerships Grow
and Develop

Chapter Three

Courtship and Commitment

Making a Good Match

He only earns his freedom and existence who daily
conquers them anew.

—*Johann Wolfgang von Goethe*

New ventures in organizational settings are always both exciting
and anxiety-provoking. The formation of partnerships certainly is
no exception. In our research we found that the simple act of considering a partnership was almost always a positive, if not exhilarating, experience. Prospective partners are often enthralled by the
idea of creating something new and, in the process, re-creating
themselves. But, while their feelings are usually similar, their reasons for entering partnerships are often quite different.

Motives for Partnering

As we noted in Chapter One, there are six primary reasons for
entering partnerships. A partnership makes sense if it provides or
expands efficiency, flexibility, resources, markets, a sense of interdependence, and personal gratification. While these six reasons
tend to sustain a successful partnership and provide valuable guidelines for determining whether or not a particular partnership is
advisable, our interviews and case studies suggest that these six reasons are usually not at the heart of people's initial decision to enter
into a partnership. Rather, this decision usually seems to be motivated by three factors, factors that tend to drive many business decisions—not just the decision to enter a partnership.

The first of these motives centers around pragmatism. This serves as the base for most of the partnerships of function that we described in Chapter Two. The prospective partners need one or more persons or organizations that can bring complementary resources to a function-oriented alliance. This pragmatism might show up as a concern for finding new markets, gaining new expertise, or obtaining greater efficiency. What these resources are, of course, can vary widely as well. Sometimes it is specific expertise, such as technical or marketing acumen. Other times it is simply money. And other times it is the ability to help extend one partner's marketing reach and, in the process, help expand his or her business horizons.

The second motive, often associated with partnerships of commitment, is much more personal. It is the need by one or more partners for more fulfilling work or a more fulfilling life-style. Frequently a driving motivation behind small-business partnerships and highly entrepreneurial partnerships among medium- to large-sized corporations, for example, is a personal need to get out from under the weight of hulking corporate bureaucracies. For people in large corporations, such partnerships provide breathing room and freedom. At other times their thinking is much more preemptive. Rather than getting out from under oppressive situations, prospective partners simply want to create a more attractive environment within a large, potentially dehumanizing workplace. Their desire for flexibility and personal gratification is often interwoven with this desire for greater freedom and control.

The third motive is intensely personal and is clearly related to partnerships of commitment. Some people want to become partners simply because they enjoy the partnership experience. This third motive is intimately tied to the personal gratification factor in partnerships. Partners find it more satisfying not only to share risks but also to share respect, give-and-take, ideas, goals, and—especially—hopes.

Pragmatism: In Search of Complementary Resources

Many of the men and women we interviewed told us that they had first considered partnering purely for business reasons. Sometimes they found partnerships of agreement that asked little of anyone in the partnership. We spent little time studying these partnerships. Often these people need another person or organization to share the costs or financial risks of starting or expanding a business, but they don't want to lose control by selling stock or depending too heavily on venture capital funding—that is, they are looking for a purely function-oriented partnership. In the case of large corporations, recent demands for very expensive technology has often driven these organizations toward partnerships.

At other times, people or organizations contemplating partnership need specific talents or expertise that they can't afford themselves; they don't have the money for new employees (even temporary or part-time) or to hire consultants. At still other times, a business simply grows beyond its organizational capacity— whether the organization consists of one person or a host of employees. Those contemplating partnership know that they can expand their organization by adding more people; however, they want to be sure that the person or people who will be running the enterprise with them are just as committed to long-term growth and stability, or else they want to connect with an existing organization with a successful track record rather than building a whole new organizational unit from scratch.

One interesting example of partners who joined forces to share costs while still retaining independent control of their business is the alliance between BiChip and TechnoCorp. (Note that in this case, as in many others in this section, we have chosen to use pseudonyms to protect the identity of the partnerships being described and discussed.) BiChip and TechnoCorp share an increasingly popular kind of arrangement called an "intrapreneurial" partnership. BiChip is a small, independent company with twelve employees.

Yet it is partially subsidized by TechnoCorp, a semiconductor man-ufacturer with more than $1 billion in annual sales. This arrange-ment can be likened to a mother suckling her young until it is old enough to fend for itself. A major benefit, of course, is a greater assurance of success. Just like a newborn, a newly created partner-ship stands a much better chance of long-term survival if it is prop-erly nursed through its first months or years.

BiChip is the brainchild of a small group of technologists, all of whom knew one another and had worked together in other compa-nies. They wanted to start a company without giving away equity or power to venture capitalists, the compromise most high-tech start-ups now make. Ironically, as they began to explore alternatives they brought in a venture capitalist, who was also a former employee of TechnoCorp, to help them in their brainstorming. He suggested that they explore a relationship with TechnoCorp, which was looking for the kind of design tool that BiChip wanted to take to market. He thought that TechnoCorp might be interested in helping to fund the start-up in a different way, perhaps as a sponsor or limited partner that could eventually make use of BiChip's product.

The idea found an appreciative audience. TechnoCorp was quite interested in the design tool and agreed to provide limited funds for a small equity position as well as office space and loaned personnel to get the venture going. In return, TechnoCorp was granted reduced license fees and a special royalty arrangement as part of its agreement to purchase BiChip's first product. In addition, TechnoCorp was given a role in developing this first product. This meant that it could participate right from the beginning in the unique position of partner, sponsor, and customer. As well as pro-viding the funds to nurse it along initially, the agreement also allowed BiChip to go out into the marketplace with its own product after the first proprietary product had been delivered to Techno-Corp. Here, again, it's irresistible to compare TechnoCorp to a responsible parent who not only nurtures but knows when to step back when the child wants to leave the nest.

Often, too, we found that the key complementary resource in a function-oriented partnership is not investment dollars but the professional expertise a partner can bring. This is clearly the case with the Tenafer Consulting Group and Franklyn University, who are about to embark on a partnership in which the Tenafer Group will offer internship opportunities for graduate students at the university, while the university will provide both credibility for Tenafer and low-cost assistance from both the graduate students and the professors who supervise them. In addition, Tenafer will provide ample opportunity for the Franklyn faculty to learn more about working in the "real world," while the Franklyn faculty can provide the professional staff at Tenafer with some of the most recent, cutting-edge concepts in their field.

Another, often related, asset is the ability of a function-oriented partner to successfully bring another partner into entirely new markets and, in effect, greatly extend the other partner's reach. One intriguing example of this is a partnership formed between American Business Services (ABS), a minority-owned and -operated management-service company, and Travelers School Services in the late 1980s to provide contract food service management for large, urban school districts.

At the time, the market was considered wide open to both ABS and Travelers. Less than 10 percent of all school districts in the United States were contracting out their food services to independent vendors. In addition, budget restrictions and government regulations were making it more difficult for school districts to continue managing their own services. The idea to break into the market was first advanced by Al Demitt, the head of ABS. He approached Travelers with a plan that he felt offered significant benefits to both organizations. Travelers immediately saw the opportunity. It clearly had the capital and other resources it needed to enter this market. But it also recognized that it lacked the level of minority representation it needed to receive a food service contract, a prerequisite in many of these urban districts. This, Demitt contended, was where he and

ABS could be of value. And Travelers agreed to the partnership.

The arrangement turned out to be a very attractive selling point. While the agreement to create "Urban Food Services" was still being drafted, a large urban district ("Metro") in a major West Coast city put its food service contract out to bid. Demitt presented the new partnership, with its combination of minority representation and ample resources, as the ideal choice, and the partnership was awarded the contract. Metro Unified became one of the largest school districts in the United States to hire an independent food service provider rather than manage its own.

Metro Unified was a visible, and challenging, beginning for Urban Food Services. The district is located in a very dangerous urban area. Drive-by shootings, gang wars, vandalism, and theft are commonplace. The business manager wore a bullet-proof vest to work every day. Needless to say, it was an environment very different from other districts Travelers had served.

Despite the newness of the experience for both ABS and Travelers, the venture worked smoothly and ended only when the school district could not pay its bills. In August of 1992, Urban Food Services left the district. Despite the financial losses, both ABS and Travelers believed that the experience at Metro was a positive one. It proved that two very different organizations could successfully partner to access a new market. And it allowed them to learn a great deal that will be applied in their next venture together.

What especially struck us about this case are the choices each partner made when considering the prospect of entering a new market. Because Travelers lacks sufficient minority representation, it is obviously not the ideal company to serve large urban school districts. So, rather than trying to change internally in order to take advantage of an opportunity, it chooses to partner with an organization that supplies its missing ingredient. In this case, a partnership represented a faster and easier route. For Demitt, the issue was quite clear-cut. He needed the resources of a large organization in order to enter the target market. So, rather than driving ABS into debt and taking total responsibility for a large-scale operation, he simply found a partner—once again, a faster, easier, and more appealing route.

A second example of a function-oriented partnership is international in scope: Visa International. Visa traces its roots back to the Bank of America, the California-based financial services giant that introduced the "credit card" in the late 1950s. The Bank-Americard was not a "charge card" like Diner's Club or American Express: instead it offered the user a revolving line of credit. If the cardholder wanted to take more than one month to pay, he or she now had that choice.

After just a decade, the Bank of America realized that the idea had global potential; after all, the card became more and more attractive to users as increasing numbers of merchants honored it. Not only could consumers use their card for a greater number of local purchases, but they could also use the same card while traveling. To help realize its vision of global utility, the bank helped establish an industry association that would license this credit card to any financial institution that met certain member requirements. Within a few years, this association took the name Visa.

Today, Visa is by far the most popular and widely accepted payment card anywhere. In 1994, more than 330 million cards were in circulation, honored at 11 million merchant locations in more than 240 nations, territories, and possessions around the world. In fact, many people in the financial services industry have remarked that Visa is the closest thing the world now has to a true global currency.

One of the main reasons it has achieved such broad global acceptance—perhaps the defining reason—is Visa's partnership-driven structure. It is not a company in a traditional sense, but an industry association, owned and directed by more than eighteen thousand member financial institutions around the world. These owner-member-partners play two unique roles: first, through various joint advisory committees, they develop Visa products and services; second, they function as their own Visa distributors. All Visa cardholders and merchants are customers not of the association but of these members. In fact, each member is a complete Visa producer that controls all aspects of its Visa program.

For these reasons, Visa sees itself not as a multinational company but as a "multidomestic" organization. It is not a company, based in one country, that controls foreign subsidiaries. Instead, wherever it is distributed, it is a local brand that is locally managed and locally owned. To help coordinate local and global issues, these eighteen thousand members in turn created another partnership—a two-tiered support organization dedicated to realizing their vision of Visa as the "preferred method of payment in the world." Visa International looks at the business from a global perspective, overseeing product- and electronic-systems development, two efforts that must be consistent worldwide to provide true global utility. Complementing Visa International are five semiautonomous regional organizations, each serving a different part of the world. Directed and advised by boards made up of local members, these organizations tailor products and develop marketing programs for each region.

Personal Fulfillment: In Search of a New Life-Style

In addition to purely business-driven reasons for considering partnership, a large number of the people we surveyed spoke—often quite passionately—about their desire for more fulfilling work or a more fulfilling life-style. These people tended to be drawn to partnerships of commitment. The particulars often varied. Some wanted to work in a more egalitarian work environment, rather than a stratified one. Others wanted more freedom to develop and explore their ideas. Others wanted to create a work environment based on certain values they cared about. And still others wanted to connect more closely with the communities in which they lived. But, despite their differences in these particulars, they almost universally shared a dislike for the traditional hierarchical organizational model. As well as their being a hindrance to professional growth and career advancement—a common complaint about large hierarchical companies—a large number of correspondents communicated two additional problems.

The first was a growing lack of job security. Up until a relatively short time ago, life-time job security was a given in many large organizations. Employees might have grumbled about dim-witted bosses and slow-as-molasses bureaucracies, but at least they had a secure job. Today, of course, this is no longer the case. As organization after organization in both the private and public sectors have "downsized," "restructured," and "rightsized" for the 1990s, job security has slowly but surely become a thing of the past. As a result, there's less resistance to striking out and taking a risk in a partnership. The second, according to several respondents, was a lack of connection with, and lack of responsiveness to, the communities in which these organizations exist. For them, work and community needed to be integrated rather than separate. And for them the need was strong enough to choose the often risky, committed partnership path. We found this to be particularly common among many of the women we interviewed, who were looking for alternative ways in which to work in a business environment that has until recently been defined primarily by men operating in traditional masculine roles.

Many of these women indicated that they were frustrated with the isolation and confinement that exists in the companies they worked for. The particulars of their cases revealed a significant difference between the women and most of the men we interviewed. Not only did the women feel thwarted by a stifling supervisor or environment, but they also felt that their careers had hit a dead end. They are examples of the kind of professional Hardesty and Jacobs describe in *Success and Betrayal* (1986), their study of corporate women. A growing number of talented female executives and mid-managers have found that they can best cope with the proverbial "glass ceiling" by moving horizontally out of the strict confines of the corporation, into a collaborative environment where the glass ceiling isn't dominant—that is, the world of partnerships of commitment.

When we began our interviews we expected that personal and professional fulfillment would be a major factor driving many family- and friendship-based partnerships. What surprised us as we compiled our interviews was how much this was also a factor in many strictly business-based partnerships. The hunger for a more satisfying work experience appears to be an enormous one for increasing numbers of people.

One issue that fascinated us concerned the number of people who considered partnerships of commitment in order to work in an environment built on specific values important to them. We found that the creation of a better community environment and the forging of closer community ties was not exclusively a motive of small mom-and-pop companies. It also was a motive in much larger, visionary corporations as they created partnerships with other firms and agencies in their own community.

A particularly interesting example is offered by the case of the partnership between Jones and Devonshire, a very innovative manufacturer of garden tools, and the Mid City Sheriff's Department. This community service–oriented partnership was formed during the early 1990s. Susan Kilpatrick, from the sheriff's department, was the partnership's prime mover. Throughout the department there had been a widespread concern that inmates were not properly rehabilitated before being released back into the community. Susan, especially, was sadly aware of the "revolving door" syndrome and the inability of government to provide these inmates with the proper tools to succeed in the outside world. Her goal was to provide the means for these people to build higher levels of self esteem, respect for others, and skills that would enable them to begin again in the world in a positive way.

With this in mind, she approached Jones and Devonshire and proposed the Garden Project at the Mid City Jail. As well as providing tools and materials, Jones and Devonshire would also provide volunteers who would assist in various aspects of the program. This ranged from offering advice to conducting actual job training for inmates. After the initial success of the program, other partners have been added, including a nationally known restaurant and a gourmet food store. A garden has been planted in a vacant lot near one of the store's facilities. There inmates grow vegetables and fruits for resale to both the store and the restaurant. And, in the course of the partnership, a limited number of jobs have also opened up for inmates after completing their sentences.

The value of this arrangement for Susan and the sheriff's department are obvious. Inmates learn new skills and work on projects that can lead to jobs after their release. In the process, they also become more accustomed to working as team members in constructive efforts. What intrigued us more was the value for Jones and Devonshire. The people interviewed spoke about benefits such as achieving broader market visibility and reducing crime in the community. But the underlying reasons, we believe, can be traced back to Jones and Devonshire's beginnings during the early days of environmental awareness in the 1970s.

Since that time, the company has had a very clear mission: to encourage a close, environmentally sound working relationship with the land. And since that time, the company has also been a leader in environmentally conscious activities such as organic gardening and recycling. With this kind of tradition, the Garden Project at the Mid City Jail was a natural. It supported the process of helping people develop healthy relationships with the environment. By caring for the land, respecting it, and working to improve it, inmates developed a new and far more positive perspective about their environment—one they could naturally extend into their interpersonal relationships.

What intrigued us as well was how the combination of Jones and Devonshire's commitment and the initial success of the project acted like a magnet to attract other businesses. Companies of all kinds are often criticized for their "lack of sensitivity" toward their local communities. But rather than being insensitive, we wonder if companies aren't primarily cautious. Once the Garden Project had experienced initial success, the restaurant, gourmet food store, and then a stream of other businesses were happy to come on board. These businesses certainly don't see themselves as callous or insensitive to the community. But it's unlikely that any of them would have made a commitment to this effort without the initial involvement of a company of the size and stature of Jones and Devonshire.

Many corporations have formed similar partnerships through their corporate services division or a company-supported foundation. The Tandem Corporation, for instance, a manufacturer of computers, offers a variety of community services in partnership with state and local government and schools, focusing on lifelong learning, dependent care, and transportation (Del Prado and others, 1992). Given that Tandem, like most other American corporations, cannot or does not want to own schools or human service agencies—nor, for that matter, does it have the expertise to run these organizations—it must work in partnership with people and institutions that have authority and expertise in these areas if it wishes to provide these services to the community.

Personal Enjoyment: The Exhilaration of Partnering

While great attention has been paid to the practical benefits of partnering in recent years, one of the fascinating discoveries for us is the degree to which many people really and truly enjoy the experience of partnering—especially in partnerships of commitment. More than just providing a chance to mesh complementary resources or to create a less stifling or more egalitarian working environment, partnerships can be downright exhilarating. The comparison between professional partnerships and marriage has been overused. In fact, we were tired of it even before we began this book. But, as we heard this comparison made in interview after interview, it began to take on new life for us. It touches on the basic power and appeal of partnerships. Like a bad marriage, there are few things worse than a bad partnership. But, like a good marriage, a partnership has the potential to provide a sublimely satisfying experience with a strong spiritual component.

It is no wonder, then, that a significant number of the people we interviewed considered partnership in ways similar to how many of us consider marriage. They may have been able to make a satisfactory living on their own, but they chose not to. They wanted to be in a partnership of commitment primarily because they enjoyed the experience and preferred the at-work life-style. In particular, they liked the experience of sharing not only risks and responsibilities but also ideas, goals, hopes, and dreams.

One quite fascinating example of this kind of thinking is found in the case of Marilyn and Kathleen, two women with separate management and career development consulting firms who have entered into a partnership together. What intrigued us most at first was what also intrigued our research associate, who interviewed them for this study. Our associate first met Marilyn and Kathleen when they jointly accepted a consulting project at her company. During the effort, our associate was particularly impressed by how—during difficult times as well as smooth—the two always seemed to be having fun. This attitude infected other members of their organizations as well. When staff members from Marilyn's and Kathleen's firms worked together, they seemed to genuinely enjoy each other's company. When they were together, they never seemed to view work as work.

Marilyn and Kathleen met in the late 1970s and have since joined their two consulting firms in a loosely structured partnership. They have no formal contract binding them. When situations warrant, they work with other firms instead of with each another. But both Marilyn and Kathleen are quick to emphasize that, despite the seeming looseness of their arrangement, they are always there for each other. Marilyn, in particular, believes in "teams of two." Ever since she can remember, she told our interviewer, she has felt that she is more creative and successful in her efforts when she isn't alone. In fact, when she was working on her doctorate degree, she actually hired a person to listen to her practice for her oral review.

Even so, everything between Marilyn and Kathleen and their two firms isn't always harmonious. "When we have a conflict," Marilyn confided, "we walk and talk and get it out. It never lingers overnight." "We may fight about perspectives or have different ideas about how certain products should be used," Kathleen added. "But there is never a difference over roles, loyalty, or control. In fact, there's never any ego or competition involved."

Marilyn made another point that, in its own way, acknowledged the close—almost spiritually linked—relationship their consulting firms share. "There are times when we literally finish each other's sentences," she said. "We know what's in each other's head. There have been occasions when this has led to such positive client interaction, we could have flown the plane home ourselves!"

In summing up this interview with Marilyn and Kathleen, our associate drew an analogy that helps to give a deeper understanding both of the extremely close bond the two partners share and the joy that naturally emanates from it. It is not an analogy to marriage but to a pair of lovers who live together without a formal marriage license. While not bound together legally, their union is certainly as strong and deep as the most committed of marriages. As a result, it is not a partnership based primarily on business considerations (a partnership of function) but, in the interviewer's words, it is "an alliance of the heart" (a partnership of commitment).

What about in much larger corporations? Do "alliances of the heart" exist in these organizations, or are such alliances found only among much smaller organizations? Certainly the alliance discussed above between the sheriff's office and the garden tool company, for example, involves more than just community concern. It is a project that activates people, that plays to their best motives, that makes them proud to be associated with a company that cares. Major corporations such as IBM have for many years donated the time of senior executives to community agencies and collegiate institutions, not only because it is good PR, but also because these senior executives come back to their job revitalized and filled with new insights regarding the operations and purposes of the corporation. Partnerships of commitment, in other words, can bring people back to life, whether they are starting a new business or continuing to work in a large, longstanding corporation.

Selecting a Partner

Partnerships always require some risk-taking. Just as a marriage inevitably requires a leap of faith, when each person is ready to trust the intentions and competencies of the other, so too does a business partnership. In this phase of discovery, the people involved have the opportunity to move beyond the initial attraction and romance and begin to define the major issues and dynamics of the relationship. In our studies, we found repeated examples of partnerships that failed or were seriously troubled because the start-up phase was never addressed and/or completed. We have much to learn therefore from the stories of start-up and commitment, and from the lessons learned by those who took the plunge.

Responding to Needs and Exploring Opportunities

Karl Bursch and Daniel Trovick each own and serve as CEO of medium-sized food companies. They have also formed a gourmet foods partnership. Karl owns a company that specializes in meats and poultry, while Daniel's company specializes in produce. They sell their products independently, but also jointly own a store and coordinate much of their advertising and special promotional campaigns. They have both previously been partners in failed partnerships. They brought the lessons that they learned from their failure to their new joint enterprise and benefit from what might be called a "strong community of memory." Karl and Daniel have chosen to learn from their mistakes and try again.

Each of these partners has genuine respect for the considerable expertise and resources that the other partner brings to the joint enterprise. In choosing to work together they know that they must be able to make extensive use of each other's strengths as the foundation for their partnership. All the *complementary* strengths in the world won't be of much benefit to either partner if they don't use them. They have also learned to set aside certain domains where each partner's company can freely roam without major interference from the other. Daniel's company, for instance, tends to emphasize the healthy properties of fruits and vegetables and produces a health-oriented newsletter each month. Karl's company does not participate in this activity, though Karl personally is very concerned about the health issues associated with eating meat.

Areas in which they do cooperate center on their complementarity. Karl, for instance, has a very experienced marketing and advertising staff who enjoy and are particularly skillful at laying out newspaper advertisements and working with newspapers to obtain good ad spots. Conversely, Daniel's staff is particularly interested in and competent at setting up displays and decorating their jointly-owned store during various holidays.

This doesn't mean that Karl and Daniel don't have conflicts. Yelling matches and rivalry are evident in their discussions on frequent occasions. However, they see such conflict as a good thing. Conflict provides an opportunity to get things out in the open. They agree that conflict is not something to be avoided. Having learned painful lessons in their previous partnerships about the cost of isolation and poor communication between partners, Karl and Daniel have set aside several hours every Saturday to discuss their two businesses and their responsibilities in the partnership. They see their roles very clearly now and have started this new partnership with more structure in place than was the case with either of their previous partnerships. Karl and Daniel are very successful in part because they have not replicated the mistakes of their previous partnerships; instead they have chosen to be particularly thoughtful with regard to roles, responsibilities, communication, and collaboration.

Given that Karl and Daniel could learn and benefit from their past mistakes, can other potential partners benefit from the lessons learned (from success as well as failure) by the partnerships described in this book? What in general do partners have to say about such issues as compatibility, trust, and prepartnership agreements?

As we compiled our interviews, we found that partnerships most often succeeded or failed not because of some readily identifiable "tangible" such as funding, technical expertise, or marketing savvy, or even on the basis of the quantity and quality of energy and resources each partner brings to the partnership. Rather, the key ingredient in success or failure inevitably had to do with the inter-personal relationships found in the partnership. Like the team of Spencer Tracy and Katharine Hepburn, partnerships succeed when the partners "click" in a certain way. This doesn't necessarily mean that electric sparks have to fly, as they did with Tracy and Hepburn. But it does mean that there has to be some kind of meaningful con-nection. The partners need to share something more than the basic "nuts and bolts" bargain they've agreed to. Sometimes this is an appreciation for the complementary skills or perspective a partner brings to solving problems, a respect for one's partner's "otherness." Sometimes it's common values or goals or a similar view of the world. Sometimes it's basic human qualities such as integrity, loy-alty, kindness, humor, and tolerance. Often it is a desire to learn from each other. Typically, it is a rich combination of some or all of the above.

More than anything else, partnerships are flexible processes rather than rigid products. They hold a distinct advantage over other organizational forms precisely because they can be shaped and reshaped by the partners in response to the turbulent conditions of our contemporary world. In order to achieve this flexibility and responsiveness, partners must be able to freely and easily work with one another. Specifically, there must be a sense of trust between the two or more partners.

It is important to recognize three different kinds of trust in a partnership. First, there is trust in *intentions*. We trust someone because we are convinced that they are interested in our welfare or in the welfare of the organization or project we are involved in together. Karl and Daniel displayed a noticeable trust in their willingness to let the staff members of each other's business work freely in their areas of interest and expertise. In the 1960s there was a common human relations exercise called the "trust fall" (still popular in many "outward bound"–type programs), in which someone falls straight backward into the arms of a second person. This is appropriately called a "trust" fall because the person falling backward must be convinced that the other person will break the fall. If the "catcher" is laughing or is distracted by a conversation with a third person, then the "faller" is unlikely to let go and fall backward, because at that moment she is concerned about the catcher's intentions, or more specifically about his commitment to the task of catching her before she hits the ground.

Second, there is trust in *competency*. We may be convinced that someone is looking after our interests, but we might not be convinced that they have the skills, knowledge, or experience necessary to benefit us or our organization. Karl and Daniel picked one another because they knew that each partner's company possessed certain competencies that were needed to make the other's business successful. Returning to the "trust fall" example, I might be convinced that the person catching me is filled with good intentions; however, if I weigh 250 pounds and the person catching me weighs only 110 pounds, I am likely to be reticent about falling backward. I might crush the person and ruin my back.

Third, there is trust in *perspective*. We may be convinced that someone is interested in our welfare and is very skillful in what they do; however, we may be concerned about whether they see the world in the same way we do. Karl and Daniel had both experienced failure in previous partnerships, in part because they never confronted their partners. As a result of these failed partnerships, they now share a commitment to confrontation and a willingness to let conflict emerge and be successfully resolved. If the person assigned to catch me during a "trust fall" is from another country or has missed the explanation of the exercise, then I might rightfully be concerned about his whole orientation to the exercise. Does he really appreciate what he is about to do? What is his attitude about this type of exercise and, more generally, about following directions? Trust in a person's perspective is much harder to define than trust in his or her competency or intention. When this type of trust is absent, we often feel vaguely uncomfortable, yet we may not know why. But it is a particularly critical form of trust, especially for partnerships composed of people from different cultures or socioeconomic backgrounds.

Finding or Creating Appropriate Partners

While these generalizations regarding trust seem like they would apply more to small partnerships, we were amazed to find that they apply just as much to large, organizational partnerships. Like individuals, organizations have personalities, values, specific ways of looking at opportunities, and other attributes that make up what is known as organizational "culture." And they can clash just as fiercely as two people in a small business. A strong sense of trust is just as important in large-scale partnerships as it is in partnerships between two individuals.

The successful joint venture between Corning and CIBA-GEIGY illustrates this point quite well. Before forming the partnership, representatives of the two companies spent more than two years planning for it. While part of this effort focused on establishing specific rules and performance requirements for the alliance, a good deal of additional time was spent getting to know each other, learning about the other company, and continually asking if the values, culture, and goals of the companies were compatible. This effort, the partners agreed, was well worth it, providing all involved with a clearer sense of just what they would be in for when they actually became partners (Lei and Slocum, 1991).

In addition we found that, while issues such as personalities, values, and outlook are extremely important, they are often given scant consideration or even overlooked altogether when a partnership is formed. Sometimes this happens because prospective partners are not sufficiently aware of just how critical these issues can become. Other times potential problems just aren't detectable at this early stage. And still other times, we believe, prospective partners—passionately wanting the alliance to work—simply refuse to see potential areas of friction.

An example of this situation occurred a few years ago in a joint venture between AT&T and Olivetti of Italy, which joined together to produce personal computers. In their haste to get a jump on the market, the two quickly agreed to the alliance. But, after they had already committed, they discovered major differences in their management styles, corporate cultures, and missions—differences they'd failed to explore adequately before making the partnership commitment. Eventually the partnership was formally dissolved (Lei and Slocum, 1991).

Why do people or organizations seek partnerships with certain people and organizations and not others who might—on paper—be equally qualified? The reasons vary almost as widely as the people and organizations attracted to partnerships. Furthermore, just as the six reasons for establishing a partnership (from Chapter One) may be overlooked in favor of the three motives identified earlier in this chapter, so can they be overlooked when searching for the perfect partner. In our research we isolated the four preoccupations that most often dominate the selection process: (1) the desire for what is familiar rather than what is unfamiliar, (2) the desire to work with like-minded people, (3) the desire to hold exclusive or at least consistent access to scarce or valuable resources, and (4) the desire to learn from a partner willing to share expertise. Each of these preoccupations can either be appropriate or inappropriate for a specific partnership.

The Familiarity Factor

We found that, in most cases, familiarity is a major reason for selecting prospective partners or for choosing partnership as the preferred way to satisfy a business need. Not only do partnerships provide the cornerstone for many business relationships, they often result from them as well. This was obvious in nearly all the family- and friend-based business alliances we studied. This is equally true, although perhaps not quite as obvious, in large organizational partnerships. We often found that the leaders of large corporations decided to partner with one another because they already knew each other from various professional and social settings. In addition, we found that experience in an existing partnership seems to both ease and expedite the process of establishing new ones: partnerships beget partnerships. This is a very understandable result of successful partnerships—people partner once, it works, so they're open to doing it again.

The Quest for Kindred Spirits

Many of the people we interviewed discussed the importance of pairing with others who share similar values, goals, and viewpoints. Most often these partnerships are extensions of existing couples or of family or friendships, or they are established in conjunction with volunteer-based enterprises.

Shared values are particularly important in partnerships between people or constituencies that are potentially in conflict. The Youthful Spirit program certainly qualifies in this regard. Established as an effort to reduce drug abuse among teenagers in a western suburban community, the program was directed by a youth board and an adult board serving in an advisory role. The complex and potentially contentious relationship between these two boards was anchored by seven basic agreed-upon guidelines, to be exhibited through actions and not just words: (1) the adults would be consistent and constant in their high level of commitment; (2) the youths would be equally committed to this unique program; (3) the staff running the program would demonstrate their commitment to the community's youth; (4) management would risk and provide room for innovation, allowing a high-involvement program to develop; (5) a well-focused mission would be formulated to keep the program on track; (6) leaders of the program would use and model good communication, so that all program constituencies would have recent and accurate information; and (7) roles would be flexible, yet they would also be clear at any one point in time. These guidelines would seem to be of value as anchors for virtually any partnership.

Indeed, we found many business-based partnerships that considered these issues to be equally important. It's interesting to note, too, that—as with AT&T and Olivetti—several of these business-based partners admitted that they'd come to fully appreciate the importance of shared values, goals, and viewpoints only after their partnerships were well under way or in the process of breaking up. As one disgruntled partner told us: "Being a partner in a business makes being married seem easy."

The Quest for Scarce and Valuable Resources

While we firmly believe that common interests, values, goals, and perspectives are ultimately what makes or breaks most partnerships, we still do not want to minimize the importance of complementary resources. Even the most harmonious of families, best of friends, or most respectful of business associates cannot make partnerships work entirely on what they share. Every partner needs to represent a unique dimension of some kind. If not, then his or her value to the joint effort will sooner or later be brought into question, especially if it is a partnership of function.

In our research we found many cases in which prospective partners took special care to seek out people with appropriate resources to offer. They needed special skills and materials not everyone could provide. Prospective partners often must look for a special product, distinctive expertise, or a unique perspective in a specific person or organization: the partnership is formed because one person or organization depends on another. Occasional access to these valuable resources is not sufficient. A special product, expertise, or perspective might not always be available or priced at a level that the party can afford. Therefore a formal (or at least semipermanent) mutual commitment is sought.

One partner may need someone with engineering or leadership expertise to assemble a group of designers to create a new computer or a new chip. Another partner may need the library holdings of a sister college or the hard-won experience of physicians in a neighboring hospital. Or a partnership might be formed to blend the sales expertise of one company with the unique marketing position of another.

Learning from a Partner

In addition to finding a compatible partner or a partner that can provide needed resources, some of the people we surveyed expressed a strong desire to join forces with someone they could learn from. This was particularly likely in partnerships of commitment. Often the reason is to learn about a specific facet of work a prospective partner has expertise in. A clear example of this is the partnership between American Business Services and Travelers School Services. The partnership's prime mover, Al Demitt, clearly wanted to know more about the school food service business, and Travelers was a leader in the area. During the partnership's first joint venture, Demitt and his ABS employees were able to observe firsthand what Travelers brought to a school operation. His experience with Travelers could very well provide Demitt with the preparation he needs to someday run a school food service operation all by himself.

Sometimes the desire is to be with people in another organization who can offer the kinds of insights and observations a prospective partner appreciates. An example of this is the "alliance of the heart" between the consulting firms owned by Marilyn and Kathleen. Not only do Marilyn and Kathleen—and, even more importantly, their two staffs—enjoy working together, they also greatly appreciate the differing perspectives offered by staff members in the other firm on various issues that come up during their joint projects.

Learning is often a major (though perhaps unacknowledged) objective of a partnership of commitment. The alliance between Jones and Devonshire and the Mid City Sheriff's Department is a case in point. Susan Kilpatrick of the sheriff's office clearly defined the partnership as an opportunity to teach inmates not only about the science of growing high-quality fruits and vegetables, but also about respect for the environment and all things living in it. Jones and Devonshire employees, in turn, learned firsthand about the problems facing inmates as they return to the world, while staff at the sheriff's office learned more about environmental concerns and strategies for addressing these concerns.

Another learning-driven partnership we found particularly intriguing exists entirely within the confines of one large utilities organization, Western State Gas and Electricity. While most of our partnership cases have focused on relationships between two or more independent organizations, it is also important to remember that units within organizations often operate in relative autonomy of one another, and that new forms of partnership between these autonomous units may be just as difficult to establish and just as important as partnerships between independent organizations.

For many years there had been a history of miscommunication and friction between two groups of WSG&E employees—its power plant operators and systems dispatchers—located together in a centralized power control facility. The operators' job is to keep the machinery at the plant running and producing electricity. The dispatchers' job is to know how much electricity the operators need at any given moment. To do this, the dispatchers also need to know how much electricity or "generation" is available from several different sources. With this knowledge they can match these various sources of electricity at any time and plan to match demand weeks and months into the future.

Despite their interdependence, operators and dispatchers might often work for years without seeing or meeting each other. This, in turn, has led many operators to view the dispatchers as "Big Brother." They call the Power Control department "Control," often cringing at the very mention of the word. These negative feelings are the result of what they see as a subordinate relationship. Often the dispatchers dictate to operators when and how they must keep their units on-line. They often question operator decisions. In fact, "Control" has the authority to reprimand operators it finds deficient in some way. Doubly frustrating to the operators is that they are under strict instructions from their boss about how to make decisions and how to communicate with the dispatchers—instructions that are often in conflict with those given by the dispatchers. To make matters worse, operators have occasionally exacted revenge on dictatorial dispatchers by making units unavailable or by making it difficult for dispatchers to get needed information.

An effort to solve this problem began when several plant operators and supervisors met to discuss common concerns after attending a leadership skills class. They agreed to approach the dispatcher supervisor with the idea of a "summit" meeting between his group and the operators. The supervisor was quite receptive. At the time, he was under extreme pressure to make his unit more cost-effective. On the one hand, he needed to find new ways to contain costs. On the other hand, he needed to do a better job of meeting the demands placed on his system. Recently there had been a number of instances when his group had barely been able to meet customer demand. Brownouts had occurred. He feared that if reliability weren't improved, large customers might go elsewhere.

Soon afterward a meeting was held to decide if an intrabusiness partnership was worth pursuing. At the meeting a planning group identified five basic principles that must be adhered to for such a partnership to succeed. First, the partnership needed support from upper management, in particular from the vice president of the Power Generation department, who could provide both time and department dollars. Second, the partnership needed to be based on personal relationships. Even though the dispatchers and the operators often talked over the phone, it was considered essential that they meet face to face to discuss ways to solve the problems that existed between them.

Third, there needed to be a focus on *how* they discussed those problems. Here, it was felt, those involved could best communicate their concerns through stories of on-the-job experiences. Fourth, technology needed to be used more effectively to provide "real-time" information. Prompt, accurate, and comprehensive information would undoubtedly be necessary to the partnership's success. Finally, the partnership—and especially the way in which it was conceived and structured—needed to demonstrate the ability to produce real and measurable cost savings.

After the partners agreed to these principles and the vice president of Power Generation committed himself to the initiative, another meeting was held. Those dispatchers and operators considered most likely to be willing to participate in such a partnership were asked to attend. The subject of the meeting was the need for more timely and accurate information exchange. The dispatchers provided "real-time" cost information and information on government regulations to the operators, explaining how and why certain decisions were made. In turn, the operators explained the problems they often had in complying with these decisions. After this the dispatchers showed a computer simulation of a system overload crisis so the operators could better understand all the factors dispatchers had to consider.

As might be expected, several valuable discoveries were made at this meeting. Many operators, for instance, had interpreted the actions of the dispatchers as signs of personal malice or indifference.

But, in frank discussion, they learned that dispatchers' motives were almost always based on the problems they were facing. They couldn't always consider one plant's needs in isolation. They didn't always have the luxury to be polite when so many different factors needed to be considered in making their decisions.

After three of these meetings, the operators and dispatchers were unexpectedly pleased with the results. Learning about the other person's job needs and perspective gave them a better sense of the entire operation; it helped them do their jobs better. Together, the operators and dispatchers began to document the savings that resulted directly from changes agreed to at these meetings. The savings came to more than $170,000. As both groups agreed, this represented only the beginning. A continuing partnership could potentially save WSG&E millions of dollars a year.

While we found in our research that the desire to learn is key to why many people and organizations commit to partnerships, we also found that it is just as often not a factor. Why? Often people's motives are complex or murky. But we believe we have identified a couple of reasons. First, some people don't consider it necessary or valuable to learn from a prospective partner. They want a partnership of agreement or of function. This thinking, in turn, can be the result of either arrogance or simply an inability to see the potential value of learning more about a prospective partner's expertise.

Second, some people don't consider learning from a partner as appropriate or even ethical. This is especially true in large interorganizational partnerships in which each party brings a very specific, very clearly defined expertise to the arrangement. A strong underlying assumption, we believe, is that learning the other party's "secrets" is somehow unethical—somehow like cheating. Perhaps this is the result of a fear many prospective partners undoubtedly have that, in an alliance, aggressive organizations will steal valuable know-how and ultimately take over a market. Perhaps these companies feel safer in an environment where no one tries to learn too much.

While it's easy to assume that such an attitude is simply "human nature," we believe it could very well be grounded in specific cultural values and perspectives. In one survey we came upon, a research team (Hamel, Doz and Prahalad, 1989, p. 138) did a long-term study of dozens of strategic alliances between U.S. and Asian companies. The team wanted to know why Asian companies generally seemed to fare better in these alliances than did American companies. Time and time again, the Asians pointed to a difference in attitudes about learning. Americans, they said, often approached partnerships with the attitude of teachers, often even trying to impress the Asians with how much they knew. On the other hand, the Asians described themselves more as students, happy to pick up whatever information they could. As one Japanese manager told the researchers: "We don't feel any need to reveal what we know. It is not an issue of pride with us. We're glad to sit and listen. If we're patient we usually learn what we want to know."

The Dangers of Whirlwind Courtships

When asked about their experience in picking partners, many of our interviewees—often themselves the survivors of unsuccessful alliances—framed their responses with cautionary notes. "If I only knew then what I know now!" one clothing retailer told us. "If I had to do it all over again, I'd do it a lot differently," an educator confided. "I just didn't do as much homework as I should have"—said an electronics manufacturer—"I should have been more careful."

While these people generally remained convinced that partnerships can be extremely valuable arrangements, they felt that the particular partnerships they had committed to were handicapped from the start. In some cases they thought they had simply picked the wrong partner. In others they believed that they hadn't satisfactorily thought through the roles and responsibilities of each party. But in almost all these cases, people felt they should have taken more time before making the commitment. More time, they believed, would have given them a better chance both to get to know their prospective partners and to design a successful working arrangement.

The reasons why whirlwind courtships often produce partnerships vary widely. In some function-oriented partnerships, for example, those involved are often flushed with excitement about the idea of together creating something new. They are often hesitant—or not cognizant of the need—to address all the tedious details that might be involved. The experience of Laura and Carol, the two women who formed the Edgewood Research Cooperative, is illustrative. These two women both head major research firms that subcontract with large American corporations. They decided to form a partnership in order to accomplish two goals: (1) to pool R&D funds for several high-risk projects and (2) to conduct several joint research projects for large corporations that neither firm could complete alone in the short period of time requested.

From the beginning, Laura and Carol's discussions regarding their research capacities and resources were fuzzy. Each was content to let her own firm do what it does well, not subjecting the mix to close scrutiny. Thus the resources and skills each firm brought to the partnership became the basis for the firms' roles. This arrangement had unanticipated consequences, however. Carol's firm, for instance, had extra space for specific research projects and had established a major line of credit, which gave it greater access to capital. The combination of these resources put her firm in an advantageous position. Soon Carol's firm began to play the dominant role, exerting greater influence than Laura's firm over decision making, defining the roles each firm would play, and so forth. This imbalance led to considerable friction, and the partnership was eventually dissolved.

But in another sense an argument can be made that the partnership was never truly formed. In their enthusiasm to venture into new fields and to grab lucrative corporate contracts, Laura and Carol set up a cooperative arrangement without explicitly discussing, agreeing to, or documenting their function-oriented partnership's mission, how resources would be allocated, and how roles would be assigned. All these issues were addressed instead by default. One of the firms simply began to fill vacuums that became apparent as the partnership evolved.

Another oft-cited reason for whirlwind courtships is external pressure. In many kinds of large business-based partnerships, for example, fast-breaking market developments make parties feel that they must commit quickly or risk missing out on an opportunity. What they don't often consider as fully as they should are the consequences of not doing it right—consequences that are usually much more unpleasant than not doing it at all. This, of course, presents a major dilemma for many potential partners. While it makes sense to take time when considering a partner, it's often not feasible. Sometimes partners must not only pick right but they must also pick fast. And, as the pace of change accelerates in today's business world and time becomes even more of a luxury, we believe this dilemma will be felt all the more keenly.

For some, especially first-time partners without the benefit of experience, a quick approach may have to be applied to the selection process. Not only will they have to be better at quickly sizing up just who their prospective partners are and what they value, but they will also have to be better at quickly sizing up just how their future alliance might work. Perhaps appropriate advice for them would be to create a vision of success for their partnership, to ask themselves, "If we were successful in this partnership, what would it look like?" Having a vision of success is one of the strongest ingredients in any effective collaborative venture.

They might also benefit from a precommitment exercise in which they ask themselves and each other a series of pointed questions. What would happen, for example, if they had a major difference of opinion about the nature or direction of the partnership? How would they deal with it? Would they talk frankly and respectfully, or would they try to avoid it? Would they take time to consider each other's point of view fully and fairly? Could they resolve the dispute in a way that satisfies them both as well as their employees, or would one of them feel compelled to impose his or her will on the other? How much would either of them or their employees be willing to bend to accommodate the other? Which issues or needs are nonnegotiable? At any rate, careful consideration—of as many factors as possible on as many levels as possible—can make all the difference in the world. While it might not assure that a prospective partnership will succeed, it will greatly improve its chances of success.

"What do I want from a partner?" In one way this is an incredibly easy question to answer. In another way, however, it can be incredibly difficult. For most people actively considering a partner, complementary resources is the first deliverable that comes to mind. They want partner companies that can provide complementary talent, expertise, or perhaps some much needed investment capital. For others, it's less cut and dried. They seek similarity rather than difference: a company that exhibits like-minded goals, values, and viewpoints. Or they seek the chance to learn: an organization that will contribute valuable knowledge, wisdom, or expertise. But for everyone serious about forging a successful alliance, the optimal partner is the person or organization that can meet all of these requirements more completely than anyone else. It often takes some time and thought to find out just who that person or organization is. But, as our interviews showed time and time again, the result is well worth the effort.

The Essential Points

1. Three motives often underlie an initial interest in partnership: pragmatism, more fulfilling work or life-style, and enjoyment of the partnership experience.

2. In exploring specific partnerships, each potential partner must trust each other partner's intentions, competencies, and shared perspectives.

3. In selecting partners, people tend to opt for what is familiar, desire to work with like-minded people, look for exclusive or at least consistent access to scarce or valuable resources, and want to learn from a partner willing to share expertise.

4. Partnerships often fail in part because insufficient time is devoted to matching the reasons for forming the partnership with the intentions, competencies, and perspectives the other partners bring to the relationship.

Chapter Four

Day-to-Day Relationship

Translating Vision into Value

Two are better than one, because they have a good
reward for their toil. For if they fall, one will lift up
his fellow; but woe to him who is alone when he falls
and has not another to lift him up. Again, if two lie
together, they are warm; but how can one be warm
alone? And though a man might prevail against one
who is alone, two will withstand him.

—*Ecclesiastes 4:9*

At the heart of the process of turning a vision into value is the effective management of the relationships that are central to any business—and any partnership. A partnership's honeymoon can last only so long. Eventually the partners must wake up to reality, including both the inevitable petty disagreements (the organizational equivalent of bad breath) and, most likely, deeply embedded differences over strategies, priorities, personnel, or any number of other issues. Partnerships inevitably involve building relationships and managing conflicts. Therefore we begin this chapter with an exploration of the ways in which partners fulfill these important roles.

Managing Relationships and Conflict in Partnerships

A partnership is successful not because the partners avoid conflict, but rather because they have found effective means of making their relationship productive and constructive rather than destructive. Successful partners discover appropriate means of building relationships and they learn to resolve conflicts that arise, so they don't fester in the background. Three ingredients seem to be critical: (1) respect for differences of opinion among the partners, (2) frequent and open communication among the partners, and (3) an underlying shared vision that helps the partners build an enduring relationship and bridge hard times.

Respect for Differences of Opinion

Respect for the people one works with is a basic tenet of most management techniques. Such respect is usually found in abundance among successful partnerships. If respect doesn't exist, the partnership probably won't get off the ground. However, even when there is a base of respect and an underlying trust between partners, they are often faced with a major challenge when differences of opinion arise over one or more central elements in the partnership.

In many cases conflicts among partners are of a type found in all organizations; namely, a conflict in values: Should we improve value or reduce costs? Do we expand our market and drive down costs through expanded volume? Do we narrow our market and increase both quality and costs? These are typical of the questions partnerships must address, and often one partner tends to fall on one side of the issue while one or more of the other partners favors the other side. Such differences of opinion can either be very destructive or they can be a source of great strength in the partnership and in the organization the partnership runs. At the heart of the matter is the respect the partners have for each other's opinions.

Frequent and Open Communication

Communication is often identified as a second key ingredient in the effective management of conflict in partnerships. Successful partnerships (like friendships) rely heavily on open, candid, and caring communication. We found—not surprisingly—that partners build relationships most effectively when they communicate with each other until they reach some understanding of the other partner's perspective. They resolve conflicts by finding a commonly acceptable solution, since neither partner can control the common enterprise without the consent of the other. Effective communication to resolve conflict requires a willingness on the part of all partners not only to advocate their position, but also to invite inquiry and to inform the other partners of their reasoning (Argyris, 1982).

As the principals in a growing partnership in the security system business, Burt and Dave speak to each other often and candidly. Burt is vice president of operations in a company that produces burglar and fire alarm systems for large corporations, while Dave occupies a comparable position in a company that specializes in devices that protect people who work with hazardous equipment and chemicals. Through their partnership, Burt's and Dave's companies often bid together for joint contracts, offering comprehensive security systems to corporations when they build new production facilities. According to Burt,

> Dave and I try to encourage each other to speak freely. We tried, you know, those every-Monday-at-eight-A.M. "get it off your chest" sessions, but we found that to be a little too formal. It kind of stifled the discussion. We both understand that we have nothing to lose by listening to each other, as well as others, and everything to gain. Dave and I want what is best for our [companies and our partnership], but at times we approach a task in different ways, and this enhances each of our growth. Between the two of us, we can have a more valid perspective and reach a desirable conclusion. You have to make a concerted effort to be open and honest with your partner.

Burt's comments illustrate three critical factors regarding the role of communication in partnerships. First, communication channels must be informal and spontaneous. Tightly structured channels block the flexibility that is so important in partnerships; furthermore, rigid communication channels don't support the partners' sharing responsibility for all aspects of the partnership's functioning. When it comes to the overall well-being of both the participating organizations and the common enterprise, there is no room in partnerships for specialized functions or clearly delineated lines of authority and responsibility. All of the partners own and are responsible for all aspects of the business. They trust one another's intentions.

Second, the partners must be truly open with one another. There is no room for secrets in a partnership, for everyone shares equally in its success or failure. Corporate executives frequently play information-dissemination games, by which they distort or even block key information as it flows from one division of the company to another division and from one executive to another. Each division and each executive tries to gain an advantage, or at the very least a fair chance at influencing the directions and allocation of resources in the company. Hence they must make "pitches," presenting their arguments in a way that often yields misinformation. Partners are not in the business of "pitching" anything to each other—if they use bad or distorted information to convince their partner to take a particular course of action, they are jeopardizing themselves and their own organization. A high level of candor is needed when you own or have assumed a major responsibility for the outcomes of a business.

Finally, Burt's comments point to the importance of the content (as well as the frequency and openness) of communication between partners. It is not enough to talk with one another; partners must also honor the diversity of perspectives and knowledge that becomes evident when communication is frequent and open. Without support for diversity, the opening up of communication channels becomes nothing more than a sham—a public relations trick. Whereas false communication is more often tolerated (or perhaps not even acknowledged) in the more formally structured corporation, it will soon be discovered and discredited in a partnership.

Shared Vision

Our interviews suggest that conflict can also be effectively defused in partnerships if there is something—like a shared vision—that is bigger than any one individual conflict and unites people despite their differences. Conflicts often seem inconsequential and readily resolvable when placed against the backdrop of some grand purpose or grand design. For example, in the case of Jones and Devonshire's partnership with the Mid City Sheriff's Department, it was reported by representatives of both parties that there has been virtually no lasting conflict, given their common commitment to a shared goal and the accompanying sense of building something significant.

Function-oriented partnerships are especially in need of a shared vision if conflicts are to be successfully resolved, for they typically don't have the established relationships or mutual commitments needed to sustain them during periods of conflict and turmoil. Furthermore, function-oriented partners often thrive on challenge and demands for creativity and innovation. Even though their partnerships are founded on pragmatic motives, these partners often have at least temporarily set aside the more mundane and bureaucratic world of a large corporation in order to take charge of a maverick enterprise; such endeavors may be especially prone to conflict.

Like many partners, Sid, of Bay Electronics, and Bertrand, of General Systech work most effectively together when there is a critical situation or a significant opportunity before them. Together they have melded Bay Electronics' ability to produce custom-made electronic products with General Systech's capacity to mass-produce certain products at very low costs. Both of these organizations thrive on competition and on internally induced pressure to succeed. At the point of maximum pressure, Sid and Bertrand set aside their individual personalities and differences in style and concentrate their efforts and creativity on accomplishing their jointly held goal of survival for both companies. They really pull together and do it! Sid feels that pressure lands them in a collaborative, nonindividualistic mode to best the enemy—whatever the enemy might be. They forget themselves for the moment and have a sense of "belonging to a bigger order." In doing so, they produce superior results.

Conversely, the Bay Electronics–General Systech partnership is least effective when things are going well and there is a low level of stress. At such times, one company might perform at a lower level than usual, having lost the crisis mentality that often seems to motivate these businesses. When this happens, Sid and Bertrand will often start comparing the contributions made by each company, and one of them will note the imbalance and his partner's lost productivity. Conflict arises, and the partnership is placed in jeopardy.

Partners must be careful not to create their own crises in order to build excitement and commitment. High-tech partnerships and others operating in highly volatile environments are particularly vulnerable to developing a pattern of "addictive" crises. Conflict is avoided in these partnerships by elevating the level of activity and increasing the number of distractions or by identifying a common enemy against whom to do battle. But in doing so, these companies often ignore the real problems that exist in the partnership. The unattended problems grow bigger and bigger, and consequently the crises must grow bigger and bigger to justify the continuing diversion of attention and resources from the underlying problems. At some point the underlying problems reach a critical magnitude and themselves become the new crisis. In this case, the enemy is the partnership itself. ("We have found the enemy and it is us!") Partnerships often blow apart at this point.

Alternatively, as was the case with Bay Electronics and General Systech, the partnership fails to cope with its own success. Once a partnership obtains a certain level of success, the partners no longer get the "highs" they had obtained by quickly and effectively responding to crises. Unresolved problems may reemerge, and they are typically much less exciting to address than the crises were. Leaders (and employees) in the companies involved in the partnership often go through "withdrawal" (anger, depression, fluctuation in moods, denial) and at least unconsciously try to create new crises to excite them again and divert their attention from the partnership's more mundane problems. Hopefully they will instead recognize this addictive pattern and focus on addressing the lingering problems in the partnership. They can then look for alternative, less destructive ways to obtain a "high," concentrating instead on their personal fulfillment and their enjoyment of the partnership life-style (a formula found in many successful partnerships).

Even in turbulent environments, high-tech partnerships need not always be undergoing profound change if the partners can anticipate market shifts and build an organization that is inherently flexible. Unfortunately, if the partners are addicted to stress and crisis, they will be inclined to create a partnership that is not structured for frequent change, and hence will always or often be in turmoil and crisis.

Partnership Maintenance

It is clear that after partnerships get up and running, partners must contend with a challenge quite different from the challenge of creation—the challenge of implementation and, in particular, the challenge of building and maintaining relationships. Often this is much more difficult than partners at first imagine. Not only does this require decidedly different talents and skills, but it may also involve the addition of new people experienced in the management of existing operations and the management of conflict. During this phase in the evolution of a partnership, several new questions must be addressed:

1. What happens now that the partnership has grown up? What kinds of changes must be made in the partnership to sustain it during its maturity?
2. How should the leaders of the partnership manage their

inevitable ongoing conflicts? Now that they know it's a long-term project, do they wish to adjust their way of relating to one another?

3. How will the partners manage the inevitable transitions in the partnership, while still preserving its distinctive features and unique advantages?

4. How will the partnership deal with major changes resulting from success, changing conditions within the partnership, shifts in the marketplace, or any number of other unpredictable events?

In addressing these questions, partners must recognize that their relationship will never be a "done deal." A partnership between two or more organizations can be compared to a pair or corp of dancers: partners moving to the same rhythm, creating a delicate pattern of ebb and flow, and, in the process, being nourished by it. Once people pair up and the partnership dance has begun, the focus turns not just to ways of working but to ways of working *together*, such that the outcome of the dance will benefit both or all involved. In the interviews we conducted, we were amazed by how often professional partners used terms to describe this maintenance phase that could also be used to describe dancers, from being "in synch" to "moving with the flow" to using "fancy footwork" to keep things in balance.

There were two characteristics in particular of this maintenance phase that seemed to be very much on the minds of many of the partners we interviewed. The first is the establishment of trust in both the intentions and competency of one's partner or partners. The second is the establishment of a delicate balance between specialization and division of labor on the one hand and the integration and coordination of functions within and around the partnership on the other. When trust and balance are achieved and maintained, then a partnership can—like a pair of linked dance partners—remain flexible without falling or being torn apart. All partners must enjoy and be nourished by the work they are doing on behalf of the partnership. Only when the work is enjoyable and gratifying will partners be able to put up with the stresses and strains associated with establishing and maintaining trust, as well as the fine balance between the specialization and integration of functions within the organization.

Maintaining Trust

Trust is often difficult to sustain between two or more people or corporate entities in our postmodern world of fragmented, temporary, and often litigious relationships. Yet, the heart of partnerships is to be found in the maintenance of trust. Critical moments in the life of a partnership often center on the formation or testing of trusting relationships. We certainly found this to be the case with the Youthful Spirit program, a partnership between a human service agency and a community advisory board in a western suburban community. The program was initially begun to promote drug awareness campaigns, but it was eventually expanded into a multifaceted drug prevention program, governed largely by young people. It makes very effective use of the energy and insight of the community's youth and the resources, skills, time, and energy of its adults.

In building this working relationship, Youthful Spirits has established a partnership of commitment between the youths and the adults. Needs are met by both groups. The youths learn skills in marketing, program design, presentation, finance, and so forth. The adults see the program as very beneficial, confronting the substance abuse problems in their community. This firm commitment between the adults and youth of Youthful Spirit was not always present. A critical event in the life of the program made all the difference in the world. In 1992, the Youthful Spirit program hosted a community support rally and luncheon. About three hundred people attended—an impressive crowd of business leaders, educators, and other community supporters. Most of the participants thought the meeting was a big success. However, at the evaluation sessions that followed a few days later, the youth involved in the program expressed their displeasure. They felt left out regarding the crucial decisions that were made in planning for the event. As a result of this meeting, a youth board was formed, with the adult board acting as its advisory. The youth board continues to have a very significant say in the direction the program takes.

Differentiation of Functions

Lawrence and Lorsch (1967) wrote nearly thirty years ago about the virtually inevitable movement of organizations toward increasing *differentiation* of functions and the concomitant need for *integration* of functions. While their model of organizational functioning seems a bit mechanistic by today's standards, the concepts they introduced are still relevant, particularly with regard to partnerships. According to Lawrence and Lorsch, as organizations get bigger and older, the tasks performed in the organization become increasingly specialized. The various units and departments of the organization tend to take on roles, responsibilities, and even cultures or styles of operation that are more and more differentiated from the organization's other units and departments.

This move toward differentiation is not only inevitable, it is also very helpful for the organization. First, people rarely are able to do everything in an organization with equal expertise and zeal—especially once the organization has become very large and complex. Second, as Emile Durkheim ([1893], 1933), the noted French sociologist, noted many years ago, specialization leads to interdependency. People remain together in organizations in part because they begin to do specific tasks and cease to be proficient (or never become proficient) at performing the other tasks the organization requires in its operations. Put simply, when there is a division of labor, people in organizations need each other! Specialization is the glue that holds them together.

Integration of Functions

It is important for an organization that is becoming increasingly differentiated to find mechanisms for coordinating its various units, departments, and functions. Lawrence and Lorsch (1967) refer to this as the process of *integration*. Any partnership that is successful over an extended period of time must move at least some distance toward differentiation of functions (though only very large partnerships need move to the level of differentiation that is typically found in large corporations). At the same time, partnerships must discover or invent mechanisms that will hold these differentiated functions together. Frequently, as Kanter (1994) noted in her own study of integration, one of the most important roles to be played by leaders in a partnership is the identification and maintenance of these integrative functions. Leadership in partnerships is often itself one of the most effective and essential integrative mechanisms in the organization.

At the South Coast Human Service Center the issue of collaboration—an integrative function—is balanced effectively with a respect for the diversity of talents that the partners bring to their partnership. The South Coast Center provides a group of independent psychologists, social workers, and rehabilitation counselors an opportunity to build a functional partnership to handle their marketing, billing, office management, and client referrals. One of the partners, Kevin, is responsible for the financial operations, while another partner, Gwen, orders most of the supplies and coordinates the joint office staff. A third partner, Trina, takes care of public relations and marketing, while a fourth partner, Randy, administers the personnel work, including staff training. Hiring decisions are made collectively.

Even though there is stability in the roles occupied by these four partners, there are two other ingredients present that are just as important to a successful partnership: a commitment to communication and a capacity for flexibility. Gwen notes that all four partners "respect each other's skills" and "are careful to consult" with each other on important matters. Kevin suggests that the partnership is constantly changing and evolving: "It doesn't fix itself at any one moment." Thus their roles do change—especially when they are busy or they are making particularly important decisions, such as moving to larger quarters. Kevin noted that there were no aspects of the new location that "hadn't been talked about." The design and its execution reflect their shared philosophy. To each of them it is a visible example of the functioning of a partnership at its best.

This does not mean that the South Coast Center partners have no problems coordinating their skills. The financial aspect of the business is still a source of stress—particularly for Gwen and Kevin. Kevin grew up on a farm, a business that has limited control over its outcomes. Thus he tends to see the center's finances in terms of fairly precise calculations. He feels "ineffective" in getting Gwen to "deal with budgets" or to develop and stay within dollar limits when ordering supplies. Her talents—for the more subjective, creative aspects of the partnership—sometimes work against Kevin's natural inclination toward the constraints he feels are necessary for good fiscal management.

Clearly the center's partners will be able to further improve the quality of their relationship and their partnership when they come to fully recognize the value of each other's perspective. Kevin described his approach as presenting the facts, from a logical, business standpoint. However, he does recognize Gwen's contributions (and the others') and indicates that the source of their disagreement resides mainly in the ongoing effort to balance creative energy with fiscal reality. Fiscal responsibility and creativity should balance off against each other—neither side should win if the partnership is to successfully adjust to the changing markets and community dynamics of their town over the next five to ten years.

Another problem concerns those moments when collaboration seems to break down. Gwen considers their partnership to be least effective when one of the partners gets into another's area and acts without consulting him or her, or neglects to consult with the other partners about activities that may affect their area of responsibility or the overall functioning of the center. Gwen says this problem is mitigated somewhat by the partners' implicit understanding that each one has veto power over the others. She stresses the importance of the other partners' really listening when one partner argues for his or her position, so that there is genuine understanding of the reasons for that position. This is clearly a partnership that places great value on the virtue and wisdom of consultation, communication, and collaboration.

The integrative function and a support for consultation, communication, and collaboration is particularly important when running an organization that is essentially voluntary in nature (see Silver, 1989). Volunteers are inclined to act on their own and to establish small, isolated cliques that are not connected directly to the overall mission of the institution they are serving. Peter Mahoney was particularly sensitive to this issue when he established a partnership with the St. Benedict church in order to raise funds for its church building project. He felt that it was critical that everybody have specific tasks to perform and that there was no interference into anybody else's area of responsibility. In supervising volunteer efforts these clear boundaries are essential, especially if the partnership is temporary, as was the case with this campaign.

Mahoney felt that his specialized relationship with Father O'Toole was also important. O'Toole was to provide knowledge about the parish and Peter was to draw up the timetable and strategy. According to Mahoney, "Father O'Toole had things to do. I had things to do. And George Shurben, the campaign chair, had things to do. It was all organized by me. It worked well because everybody followed the initial plan, which was my responsibility, and I said, 'Let us sink or swim with this.' It worked out well." Mahoney was successful precisely because he encouraged a clear differentiation of each person's functions and discouraged any crossing of boundaries, yet he also provided an integrative mechanism—in this case the initial

master plan that guided and helped coordinate all the different, isolated parts.

We suspect that the overall mission of the church and the parishioners' common commitment to the preservation of the church also
served as a guiding, integrative mechanism for this functional partnership. And there was probably yet another unacknowledged mechanism of integration at work: the trusting relationship established
between Mahoney and his clients (Father O'Toole, the parishioners,
and community leaders). Father O'Toole notes that he "had to trust
Mahoney's competence as a professional fundraiser and, in turn,
[Mahoney] had to trust my feel for the parish."

Because they trusted him, Mahoney's clients accepted his clarification of boundaries and his integrative master plan. This clarification and integration was particularly important for this
partnership, not only because most of the people working on the
project were volunteers, but also because it involved a new set of
activities for most of them. Mahoney was the only partner who had
much knowledge of fundraising activities; therefore, he set the goals,
did the training, and provided overall, integrative guidance. It was
critical, therefore, for Mahoney to be trustworthy—both in terms
of his competency and in his interest in the welfare of the church.

Mahoney acknowledges the central role trust played in this
partnership: "Yes, trust was important, . . . I suppose because the
people involved had not been in fundraising before and I had to do
a lot of the directing: setting meeting times, writing for people what
to say, scheduling events as the campaign proceeded. Later in the
campaign I took a background leadership role. I wasn't as visible to
the community. One thing, fundamentally, you have to understand
at the very beginning: everything has to be laid out, from the start
to end. No surprises." It is essential for such partnerships to remain
flexible, to allow the focus to fall increasingly on the client partner
as he or she begins to assume responsibility for solving emerging
problems without assistance from the consultant partner. If the consultant doesn't gradually disengage or shift direction during this

process, a dependency relationship is formed that can be destructive for both partners.

Not all of the partnerships we studied exhibited an effective interplay between differentiation and integration. In several instances we saw an imbalance in one direction or the other. What, for instance, might have occurred if Mahoney was to conduct a long-term fundraising effort with St. Benedict's? Would his somewhat autocratic style have still been welcomed if the fundraising volunteers had acquired considerable experience themselves? Would they have wanted as much differentiation of function, such that they would be unable to influence other aspects of the operations? Would they have been willing to let Mahoney dictate the overall master plan, or would they have wanted more involvement in this effort? Would the new mechanism of integration have been a process of collaboration and communication, rather than strict guidelines and trust in the consultant?

In virtually all the partnerships we studied, a fine balancing act was being performed—sometimes successfully and sometimes unsuccessfully—between specialization and differentiation of functions, on the one hand, and integration and coordination of these functions, on the other hand. It is usually foolish for partners simply to replicate each other's strengths and perspectives. There are often not many benefits derived from a partnership if both or all of the partners think alike and bring the same competencies and experiences to the partnership. Partners must value the distinctive contributions of each other.

Yet, there is also the need for a center that will hold the partnership together. Sometimes this integrative function consists primarily of effective leadership. At other times clear and consistent communication seems to be important. In yet other instances a common purpose or vision, such as a ritual or a strong culture, may be the key to the partnership's survival. Partners must discover their own way of integrating functions, and they should never rest easy if these integrative mechanisms are absent from their organization and their relationship. If integration is absent, then the partnership is likely to end up with nothing but alienation, anger, and disappointment.

Enjoyment of the Work

Partners are not alone in needing to find satisfaction in their work. However, partners have a greater opportunity than most people to design a work environment that they find truly satisfying. This is one of the major reasons they form partnerships in the first place—especially if they choose to risk establishing a new interorganizational partnership of commitment.

Carol and Laura of Edgewood Research certainly took their own enjoyment into account when they selected the kind of research projects they would do together. When they first began, Carol handled almost all the customer contact work, while Laura and Carol together designed most of the research projects and oversaw their implementation. Carol indicated during her interview that this was the most enjoyable period of their partnership. Both she and Laura became thoroughly enamored with the creative process involved in both design and execution of their joint projects. Like many partners, Carol indicated that she was "lost in work" during this period of time—reminding us of the "flow" experience described by Csikszentmihalyi (1975, 1990)—and was very happy with the partnership.

By 1988, each partner had drifted away from the partnership, and their firms were now primarily serving distinct client groups throughout the entire research cycle (marketing, contracting, design, implementation, and reporting of results). Carol and Laura had recognized the value of differentiation of services and the value of extended, uninterrupted work with a single client; however, they failed to recognize the need for integrative functions to balance off the differentiation. They had lost the glue in their partnership—the mutually creative design and development work—that had held their partnership of commitment together and had made it an enjoyable and meaningful enterprise for both partners.

The four partners in the South Coast Human Service Center were apparently much more successful than Laura and Carol in designing their partnership in such a way as to keep the enjoyment of their work alive. Throughout their interviews, Gwen and Kevin spoke of the deep and abiding satisfaction they derive from partnership with their three colleagues. Words such as "pleasure," "joy," and "fun" punctuated their conversations. Respect for the different skills and interests that each partner brings to human service work was expressed with enthusiasm. Both partners spoke about how they enjoyed coming to the center every day, how they always wanted to be able to do so, how they couldn't imagine what it would be like without their common enterprise. They said they had "no boundaries" between their life and work. As Kevin puts it, "If you love what you are doing, it really ceases to be work." Gwen's thoughts mirror Kevin's: "Having to be here all the time is not a restriction but a pleasure. . . . What others regard as a burden, we find a joy."

Even within the confines of large corporations, people in partnerships often find great enjoyment in their work. One of the important benefits of the service-oriented partnership between Jones and Devonshire and the Mid City Sheriff Department—and a reason for sustaining it—is the increased job satisfaction experienced by J and D employees. They feel they are part of a business that contributes to the community and supports the creation of a better environment for all. For the Sheriff's Department, the partnership creates hope, because the support comes not from a government agency or a nonprofit organization wrestling with budget cuts, but from a prospering corporation that effectively blends profits and social responsibility.

The president of TechnoCorp, the parent corporation and partner of BiChip, comments that many TechnoCorp employees were quite envious of BiChip employees because of the joy they seemed to experience in their work. They saw BiChip employees as a select group of people working on a new, exciting—even glamorous—project. They were starting a new business together—the dream of many people in high-tech companies. The president of TechnoCorp spoke about the cachet of prestige that attaches to a start-up operation or to the special group working on a secret or little-understood project. In starting its unique partnership with BiChip, the leaders of TechnoCorp were helping to create a special environment that tended to foster pride, enjoyment, and a sense of fulfillment—not bad ingredients for a new company seeking to move into a new market. The challenge was to extend this excitement (rather than envy) to employees in the parent organization.

The enjoyment experienced by the people at BiChip and the overall success of the enterprise—as is the case in many other partnerships of commitment—depends in large part on the quality of the relationships among the partners and those working in the company. We have identified employee relationships as a key component in the success of a partnership out in the world; this ingredient is critical to the internal success of the partnership as well. People seem to enjoy working in a partnership in part—often in large part—because of the sense of collaboration and "partnership" found in meeting a challenge and delivering a high-quality service or product. The president of TechnoCorp identified close, collaborative relationships as a key ingredient in the success of BiChip. Furthermore, when he was asked how the partnership between TechnoCorp and BiChip began, he focused on the intimate relationships between the players. He stated that if it hadn't been for the close personal ties between the key people, there never would have been an idea, much less a company.

The president of TechnoCorp described the rich tapestry of trust that was established inside BiChip—and at TechnoCorp as well. This trust, in turn, encouraged a willingness to take a risk on a personal word rather than requiring a written contract. It enabled a spirit of exploration, of making a good old-fashioned try (with limited funds at risk) without having to file financial reports every week

or month. As is the case in many successful partnerships, each partner learned something from the other and from the successes and
failures of the organization they had formed together. According to
the president of TechnoCorp, the chance of success for the venture
was, from the outset, predicated far more on the relationships
among the people working at BiChip (and the key players in TechnoCorp) than on the technology.

The Essential Points

1. Partnerships remain successful after the initial honeymoon if
   there is respect for differences of opinion among the partners,
   frequent and open communication, and an underlying shared
   vision that helps the partners build an enduring relationship
   that bridges the hard times.

2. Partnerships are effectively maintained if continuing attention is given to preserving trust in the partners' intentions
   and competencies.

3. Partnerships are also effectively maintained if a delicate balance is established between specialization and division of
   labor on the one hand, and integration and coordination of
   functions within and around the partnership on the other
   hand.

4. Partnerships should be enjoyable for all participating partners,
   especially given that they are voluntary; they should be sufficiently flexible to accommodate varying interests and aspirations.

Chapter Five

Transformation

Changing the Relationship or Parting Amicably

> What bitter wrong can the earth do us, that we
> should not long be here contented?
> — *Elizabeth Barrett Browning*

What happens when a partnership matures? What happens when it has to undergo major changes because of success; changing conditions inside the partnership; shifts in its markets, competitors, prices, or cost structures; changes in technology; or any number of unexpected events? The information from our interviews suggests that effective transitions within partnerships are initiated and managed when there is both acceptance of (and even enthusiasm for) the processes of change and acknowledgement of the need for continuity and broad-based support. These are the two essential (though seemingly contradictory) elements that must be present for partnership transitions to be successful.

In Sickness and in Health

In our investigation of partnerships we heard time and time again that different stages in the life cycles of organizations require different strategies, structures, systems, and competencies. Likewise, the capability to court a new alliance is often quite different from that required to build and sustain an infrastructure that continues to add value to a partnership. Redefining an existing relationship may require distancing oneself from it.

In our exploration of partnership ventures, we have come to see partnerships in terms of the capability to define and *redefine* enterprises as complex systems. By contrast, hierarchical structures are characterized by their ability to plan, manage, and control assets over time. In partnerships, "re-creation" is the operative word; in a hierarchy, it's "stability." At each stage of its evolution, a partnership is presented with an opportunity to further develop both the capabilities and the scope of the partnership. The success of a partnership is not necessarily a function of time spent together. That notion represents an old paradigm.

Hamel, Doz, and Prahalad (1989, p. 138) point out that they "did not judge the success or failure of each partnership by its longevity—a common mistake when evaluating strategic alliances— but by the competitive strength on each side." They go on to note that, from their work with fifteen strategic alliances over three years, they determined that a driving need in partnerships for harmony and cooperation has limits. They admit that "there is a certain paradox here. Alliances seem to run most smoothly when one partner is intent on learning and the other is intent on avoidance—in essence, when one partner is willing to grow dependent on the other. But running smoothly is not the point; the point is for a company to emerge from an alliance stronger and more competitive than when it entered."

The ultimate test for any organization—be it a partnership, an individually owned company, or a corporation—is its capacity to cope with the inevitable changes and stressful periods it encounters. The people we interviewed spoke most frequently of the stress associated with changes in partnership status—losing a partner, gaining a partner, or shifts in the level of one or more partners' involvement in the strategic relationship. They also described changes in the internal environment of the partnership—particularly changes associated with growth and increased complexity.

External environmental changes were cited as one source of stress. These include shifts in technology, regulations, and the community in which the partnership is located. Many partners we interviewed talked about stress associated with changing markets for the products or services they offer. These changes are often precipitated, in turn, by economic conditions and demographic changes in the communities the partnership serves. We found that partnerships are often uniquely suited to responding to changes in internal and external conditions. The special flexibility and pragmatism of partnerships are often of great value in the face of these multiple sources of change—and are sometimes sorely tested by them.

Major changes that partnerships undergo include adding partners, losing one or more current partner, changes in leadership structure, shifts in communication patterns, and so forth. We will focus first on changes that occur with regard to partnership status, then turn to changes in the internal working environment of partnerships, changes in the external needs and resources associated with them, and, finally, changes in the markets they serve.

Changes in Partnership Status

Sometimes a change in partnership status occurs almost immediately, as partners attempt to work out their initial expectations and roles. More often the change occurs later in the life of the partnership, when the realities of collaborative life sink in or, more frequently, when the common enterprise shifts in size, complexity, or direction. When a change in partnership status occurs at the very beginning, the remaining partners are usually quite relieved to have discovered and resolved the problem early on rather than later—when the negative impact would probably have been much greater. When a change occurs later, the shift is often quite disruptive. A major transition in partnership status, for instance, occurred in the food distribution partnership started by Ned Krinkoff and Bennett Thalberg. One partner withdrew after six months of operation. There is a happy ending, however, for the "prodigal" partner returned to the partnership after several years and is now an actively contributing member of the team.

Ned and Bennett each served as vice presidents for marketing in independent food producing companies. Ned's company produces canned tomatoes and tomato sauce, while Bennett's company produces gourmet pasta and rice. Ned and Bennett brought their two companies together to package and market a "full Italian meal" (canned tomato sauce plus pasta). Ned (the partner who left) describes the situation this way: "I was with the [partnership] for about six months and we had a parting of the ways, so I went to work in [a nearby town] for a while and then went overseas. . . . I've just come back, about seven months ago, from three years overseas, working as a marketing executive for [a large hotel and transportation corporation]. When I was gone they had a hard time . . . at first. I know that."

While the partnership continued between the two companies, Ned had provided an important source of expertise in marketing to a price-conscious consumer. The presidents of both companies brought in several members of their staff who had technical expertise in the area Ned had previously covered. Even without Ned, the joint venture was quite profitable—so profitable, in fact, that the two companies expanded their partnership to produce a second product line: a "full Hungarian meal."

Bennett offers a somewhat different though complementary perspective regarding the departure of Ned: "Within a year after [Ned] took off due to family problems, we really struggled and were about ready to throw in the towel. . . . We were struggling with . . . this and that, so we just said enough's enough." Bennett attributes the trouble specifically to the loss of Ned's expertise:

> At that time we had lost [Ned] . . . and [his company] replaced him two times with different people who didn't work out. Things were going up and down. We had to say to ourselves: we have certain things in line but we need to bring in a consultant who can take a step back and get an overall picture of what's going on, 'cause we had so many things going in different directions. . . . That really got

us on the right course. It got all the horses in the right corral, so to speak. With problems we work right through 'em. You really have no choice, but to work through them. Cause if you don't, you're gonna fall flat on your face.

Thus we see how, in the case of this partnership, the loss of one leader was compensated by bringing in a consultant and other employees with comparable skills. Rather than simply bemoaning the loss of their colleague or trying to replicate Ned with other employees, the companies in the partnership turned to a new, outside resource.

It is not uncommon for partnerships to lose partners at a relatively early stage. It is somewhat more painful and difficult when a partner chooses to leave at a later point in a partnership's growth and development. This happened to Sporting Generation, an alliance of four specialized sporting goods manufacturers to coordinate marketing and distribution of their products to various stores through a shared fleet of trucks. Sara, the CEO of one particular company, recalls the process of trying to resolve conflicts in the partnership and subsequently asking one of the partners to leave:

> [We tried] to iron things out, come up with general guidelines of where we wanted the [partnership] to go and ways we might be able to work together. . . . It worked for a little while, but it just didn't seem like it was going to carry us in terms of the leaps and bounds that we really wanted to make. . . . What we were after then was that there really needed to be a parting of ways, and it was really a difficult thing to do, because we were so much of a family and relationships were all intertwined. . . . Everybody felt like this was their baby. It was hard to wrench it away, [to] . . . divide the baby in quarters. And it was just so . . . personally, it was really hard to hurt someone's feelings . . . and to say to someone's face we don't want you anymore, can't work with you. . . . Since [the one partner left] it's worked a lot better.

The three remaining partners share many values in common, values that are different from those held by the partner who was asked to leave. Millie (another partner) and Sara attribute the conflicts they had with the fourth partner to these value differences. Sara illustrated the differences with a story about deciding to purchase several new trucks. Three of the partnership companies were ready to just go and do it (using their credit lines) and create the joint enterprise to pay for these trucks. But Derrick, the owner of the fourth company, wanted to save up and then purchase it. Sara explains that "we don't wait, we jump. We don't get caught up in details. . . . We look out there and see how it looks when we are done, and then we start filling in the blanks." The three risk-taking companies asked Derrick's company to leave the partnership because of their incompatible perspectives. The element of risk-taking is important in any new partnership, and, as happened to Sporting Generation, differences with regard to risk-taking have broken up many partnerships.

By far the more common shift in partnership status comes not from the departure of one or more of the founding partners but from demands on one or more partners for more time and a more active participation as a result of growth in the size or complexity of the business the partnership runs. Frequently, not all of the partner companies can commit the same amount of resources (staff, money, space, expertise, and so forth) when the partnership first starts. This can cause major problems unless the distinctive contribution made by each organization is fully honored.

Millie, of the Sporting Generation partnership, indicates that when their joint marketing and distribution system was first set up, she shared responsibility primarily by providing some additional funds (from a small reserve fund in her company) to help support the common enterprise: "We were working . . . very much like family," she says. When Millie brought her funds to the partnership (via her company's credit line) she knew that "it wasn't just mine." Millie indicated that the owners and employees in the other companies "felt like they were sacrificing something by working so many hours" developing marketing plans and setting up delivery schedules. They made little money while they were busy setting up these plans and schedules, hence they were sacrificing time (which ultimately translates into money), just as Millie's company contributed capital. The companies participating in Sporting Generation have had to adjust to the differing natures of their respective contributions.

As the individual companies grew, another transition occurred: the partnership contracted with one of its constituent companies to coordinate the trucking operation. As is the case in many partnerships, as a result of its rapid growth, Sporting Generation required greater involvement on the part of one of its partner organizations than the others. This, in turn, meant shifting roles, shifting responsibilities, and shifting perspectives for those who ran the business.

Partners, like leaders of any other contemporary organization, should be very careful about promoting growth and expansion without a thoughtful consideration of the changes that are likely to occur if this growth is successfully achieved. In any partnership, growth entails an increasing need to coordinate and integrate activities. This, in turn, requires that a greater proportion of the partnership's total resources be devoted to indirect rather than direct services (Bergquist, 1993). Costs of products therefore tend to increase, and the partnership's competitive edge is often lost.

Growth can be particularly disruptive in partnerships, because one of the key ingredients of their success is access. Partnerships provide leaders with access to the things that will keep them competitive in a changing game—things such as power, information (itself a major source of power in our postmodern world), customers, and resources (money, people, equipment). When partnerships become very large or complex, much of this advantage drops off, and the partnership becomes just another large, cumbersome bureaucracy.

Even when a partnership exists between independent organizations, it is an intimate affair; ultimately it must depend in part on the commitment of individual people to the partnership's vision. They will often have to deal with the issue of planning for succession—what will happen when one or more of the partnership's leaders move on to other ventures or other companies (as happened in the "full Italian meal" partnership)? When a transition in either membership or leadership occurs, the partnership is likely to go through a period of major stress and potential dissolution—particularly if the other original partner or partners remain. Less common, but no less important with regard to changes in partnership status, are shifts in the psychological state of leaders in the partnership.

Shifts in the personal lives of key players impact significantly on the nature and longevity of the partnership relationship. Several of the people we interviewed spoke candidly about their partnership as a source of close personal relationships they didn't find at home; alternatively, some spoke about their spouse's exceptional support of the close working relationship they had with other partnership members. Many other interorganizational partnerships similarly involve travel, as well as additional time at home studying the other partners' organization and overtime at work to keep up with the demands of both the internal and the partnership enterprise. Our interviews often revealed family tension sparked by the diverse demands imposed by partnerships. Family support is often an important ingredient—especially among the leaders of small and moderately large businesses—in a successful partnership.

The participants in a partnership of commitment must also be particularly concerned about shifting leadership roles. Partners are not simply in business together; they are committed to each other's welfare as an intimate component of their joint enterprise. They are often like family to each other. This sense of family and commitment typically extends from partnership leaders to employees of the participating organizations, even in large corporations. When they are truly effective, partnerships provide continuity and care—something that is in short supply in many postmodern organizations. While the leaders of most organizations have become increasingly distant from the cares and concerns of their employees (Sennett, 1981) and have often moved much more toward temporary relationships with their employees, partnerships of commitment can produce deep, long-term relationships.

Change in a Partnership's Internal Environment

Frequently partnerships bring on their own crises and needs for change. Crises are often precipitated not by the partnership's failures, but by its successes. A partnership growing in size must, like a growing reptile, soon shed its skin and take on another, more appropriate, structure. It might shift its focus to a slightly different line of work, or it might take on additional services and activities. Such shifts require adjustments in the strategic relationship—adjustments that can be quite stressful and can even threaten the partnership's continuation.

Our food distribution partnership ("full Italian meals") exemplifies the sort of difficult transition that comes with growth and success. In this case, expansion occurred just at the point when Ned decided to rejoin one of the two companies participating in the partnership. As Ned tells the story, his return coincided with the opening of the second product line ("full Hungarian meals") several months earlier: "Expansion is necessary if you're really going to be successful. . . . They had maxed out with ['full Italian meals'], so we decided to open the second [product line]." Bennett adds his perspective: "Opening ['full Hungarian meals'] was a major hurdle. We had hit a growth peak . . . and the next step was either staying there or expanding. We expanded out . . . and we're actively seeking a third [product line] now."

Ned adds more to this narrative of growth: "To do better, to get ahead, to make more money, we have to expand." According to Ned, you can't have unlimited income with a single product line—you can only push one marketable item so far. Bennett shares a similar vision of the future with Ned, though his vision includes a longer-term commitment to the partnership (in the form of franchise stores). His ultimate goal? To have four or five food stores that exclusively sell the various "full meal" product lines. Ned and Bennett seem, on one level, to recognize the problems associated with growth; nevertheless, they and the other central participants in the partnership dream of expansion while seemingly ignoring the fact that with additional growth they may have to become more involved in the partnership, possibly at the expense of their home companies. This is one of the seductive aspects of growth. We assume that growth will result in independence, when it is often the other way around.

Another frequent effect of rapid expansion in large and complex partnerships is unequal growth among the partnership's participants. This often causes tension, particularly if one of the partners is overseeing or responsible for those units that are growing, while another partner is responsible for the units that are not growing or are even in decline. In the case of Aaron Sinclair and Phil Lancaster, who formed a partnership between their computer rental and computer service businesses, the partnership grew rapidly in one geographic region but not in a second region. Aaron oversees the less rapidly growing region, while Phil oversees the rapidly growing region. Furthermore, Aaron manages the less glamorous and slow-growing rental business, while Phil runs the more innovative and thriving computer service organization. Aaron has let Phil know that he is not interested in being left behind. They resolved the issue by updating Aaron's business, bringing in new computer technology. Phil continues to look beyond the immediate reaches of their common enterprise, and Aaron retains responsibility for the daily operations of the partnership and continues to strive to be more up-to-date.

Despite the resolution of their personal difficulties and their commitment to a "reasonable man" method of conflict resolution (sitting in a room together and talking until the conflict is resolved), Aaron and Phil would both like to leave the partnership—primarily because they are both getting tired of the computer business. However, as they both indicated, partnerships are "easy in, difficult out." They are both very open in stating that the primary factor that is keeping them together is money. One wonders if they lost interest in the business and their partnership because Phil didn't want to show up Aaron. Aaron and Phil jointly came up with one innovative, cutting-edge idea (providing a "free technological upgrade" and service contract with all rental computers). However, since that time, Phil has been reticent about suggesting his own innovative ideas, and he seems to resent Aaron's failure to come up with any new ideas himself. Perhaps Phil and Aaron accelerated their mutual loss of interest in the business in order to avoid interpersonal envy and conflict.

Change in External Needs and Resources

While many partnerships are confronted primarily with internal changes, others find that external changes are the challenges they face most often. Like any organizational type, partnerships must be able to respond to shifts in the external environment if they are to be successful. In our uncertain times, the "closed-system" organization is a relic from the past and will soon die. This seems like a rash statement to make in a world that knows few universal truths. We make this statement because heavily bounded, highly structured, deeply entrenched organizations are simply unable to learn from their mistakes (Argyris and Schön, 1978) and lack the capabilities—what Peter Senge (1990) calls the "five disciplines"—needed to survive turbulence. The "open-system" organization, which is responsive to (and also vulnerable to) shifting resources, technologies, regulations, and general economic conditions, will survive, though only through a series of shifts and transformations in the internal operations of the organization and partnership.

Many intriguing stories were offered us regarding ways in which partnerships responded to changes in external needs. In the case of the South Coast Human Service Center, shifts in community needs and interests were particularly important, given their philosophy of integrating the center into the fabric of community life. Their locality, for instance, has experienced crime for the first time in its history. Women are less willing to go out alone at night and therefore are less likely to make use of the center's services. In response to these shifts in the community, the South Coast Center now offers programs on self-defense, as well as encouraging clients to set daytime appointments (including weekends).

Technological changes have also taken place. The South Coast Center now has access to information on CD-ROM equipment about various treatment programs, research on specific emotional problems, and new regulations and funding initiatives. This has enhanced the capacity of the individual South Coast partners and their employees to help their clients. Yet how do you keep a personal-service touch when you spend your time looking at the computer screen rather than meeting with clients? If not carefully used, the new technology could make the South Coast Human Service Center into nothing more than a mechanized technical service agency.

Governmental regulations have also affected the center, just as they do much larger and more complex partnerships. Often the four firms in this partnership have to comply with regulations and prepare governmental reports that were designed for large corporations staffed with legal and financial experts. Like many partners we interviewed, Gwen and Kevin complained about business legislation that is geared to the modern-day emphasis on bigness. Much of this legislation seems to be antithetical to effective clinical service, and it makes it difficult for a professional partnership like the South Coast Center to survive.

Gwen and Kevin talked about these many difficult external changes; they stressed the need for the four partners to keep communicating about these changes and to never assume they know what the other partners are thinking about any particular environmental change. Despite the sometimes unwanted impact of external events, Kevin and Gwen indicated that there has never been a time when their partnership was in danger of dissolving. They just never thought of not doing what they're doing! Three important things keep it together: they enjoy the business of serving human needs, they enjoy interacting with their partners, and they all recognize the economic contribution of the partnership to their lives.

Changes in the Marketplace

The external environment a partnership must face consists not only of spontaneous and uncontrollable regulations and technologies but also various aspects of the marketplace that the partnership serves. Marketplace issues include the nature and extent of the market being served, prices of the products and services being offered, and, of course, the nature and quality of products and services being offered. As organizations of all types rethink their targeted customer base and the ways in which they serve their customers, they tend to move toward various partnership arrangements or to look at restructuring the partnerships in which they now work. Customers are now more demanding, they are shrewder, and they have more information and can change their minds quickly. By providing flexibility and pragmatism, a partnership can help many businesses respond to these changes.

A successful story regarding partners adjusting to a changing marketplace is found in the collaboration between the high-tech companies Bay Electronics and General Systech. Operating in the highly unpredictable electronics industry, Bay Electronics and General Systech have faced many challenges with regard to changing markets. At one point, Bertrand (the owner of General Systech) became so frustrated with the market's unpredictable and often ambiguous conditions that he wanted to sell out his own company. Both Bertrand and Sid (the owner of Bay Electronics) knew that they were entering a field that was always turbulent. Nevertheless, they hadn't fully anticipated what was to come in becoming owners of their own business. Technology changes at such a rapid pace that they each had to constantly rethink and redefine their individual businesses. However, they have found that their partnership helps them remain flexible and open to new possibilities. Their partnership has remained market-driven and has always steered them toward new revenue and profit opportunities.

At one point Sid and Bertrand steered their partnership in a direction that produced high revenue but was very difficult for Bertrand. Their marketing strategy was to sell high-quality, low-cost, integrated turnkey network services rather than emphasizing hardware sales. It was too much for Bertrand, because his company is primarily in the business of mass production, whereas these new integrated services require much more specialized production processes. Bertrand felt that his own company's mode of production was not compatible with this new product line; hence, the work load and the level of frustration for his staff was so overwhelming that he wanted to get out of the partnership. Sid asked him if they could examine what was happening and determine what had changed. Once they had thoroughly investigated the changes, they realized that they had moved in a direction that was probably not good for either one of them in the long run.

As a result, Sid and Bertrand have re-created a partnership with more balance. It is partly driven toward integrated services and partly driven toward hardware sales. The hardware side of their partnership is now very successful and has become the strategic direction for their joint enterprise. It is ironic, because they made a deliberate and carefully considered decision to balance their joint enterprise with a greater hardware sales component, based primarily on the needs of one of the partner companies. Then they find out that the marketplace is moving in that direction too. They have niche products that do not have any real competition at this time. Sid and Bertrand changed their partnership to fit their interests, and now they are making more money then ever and they both love their partnership. As our colleague who interviewed Sid noted, they may or may not have been gentle with each other during this difficult period in the life of their partnership, but they did whatever was necessary to feed their "family" (that is, their individual companies and the partnership) and stay afloat. This is part of the genius of an effective partnership.

Terminating a Partnership

The partners we interviewed spoke not only of the distinct advantages of partnerships and the strategies needed to keep a partnership alive, but also about problems associated with the dissolution of a partnership. They noted (and we too have certainly noted) many unfortunate instances when partners have remained together primarily because it is so very difficult to dissolve a partnership once it is formed. This, in turn, speaks to the need for very careful tending of partnerships and for careful consideration as to whether partnership is really a good idea for any particular person.

From our interviews we came to the conclusion that partnerships tend to take on one of four characteristics with regard to longevity and change. In some instances, a partnership is redesigned or reconfigured in a radical manner. We have considered these changes in the first section of this chapter. A second type of partnership, invariably a partnership of function, is one that was designed from the first to be short-term. Bringing this type of partnership to a close is usually not considered a failure by any of the parties; rather, it is typically a sign that the partnership did what it was intended to do and can now go out of existence.

A third type of partnership is one that is no longer working—or perhaps never really worked very well. The partners have the wisdom to end the arrangement, or perhaps they are simply fortunate enough to have few constraints preventing them from ending it before it becomes too destructive for the partners, their employees, or the partnership's customers. The fourth type of partnership was, unfortunately, evident among our case studies as well. This is a partnership that is not now working and has not been working for quite a long time. For one or more reasons, however, the partnership cannot be brought to an end. In some instances these reasons are quite appropriate and the partners must continue despite their difficulties. These situations speak to the care that must be taken before beginning a partnership, given the frequent difficulties associated with dissolving these relationships. In other instances the reasons for keeping the partnership going are not very persuasive and are often quite irrational. The partners in these cases often need some outside assistance to disengage emotionally and personally from the destructive bind that holds the partnership together and captures the partners in a nonproductive relationship.

We will consider each of these types of partnerships in turn and suggest several ways the issue of termination might be handled in each case.

Short-Term Partnerships

When most of us think about partnerships, we envision long-term commitments—"till death do us part." There are in fact many short-term partnerships that play a significant role in the functioning of many organizations and interpersonal relationships. We can look around us and discover many short-term relationships among temporary partners: the moving company that packs and transports household or company goods; the psychotherapist who establishes a "therapeutic alliance" with his client; the architect who designs a new home or office; the CPA who conducts a company's yearly audit; the local housing coalition a neighbor joined to get a local ordinance passed by the city council; even the special relationship established between the audience and the actors and actresses who jointly create a temporary environment for the willing suspension of disbelief.

Certainly one of the most common forms of temporary partnerships is the consultative relationship. Consultants and clients form temporary partnerships to solve problems, make difficult decisions, and plan for the future. Consultative relationships are often successful precisely because they are nonhierarchical and temporary—thereby allowing the consultant to freely offer his or her advice, insights, or discomforting evidence without fear of losing his or her job or substantial funds.

The consultative relationship between St. Benedict's parish and Peter Mahoney, a professional fundraiser, exemplifies this type of short-term partnership. In essence the partnership had four members: Mahoney, Father James O'Toole, the parishioners, and the local community. The actual fundraising campaign began in late January and ended in March, though the planning and preparation had begun a year earlier. The objective of the campaign was to raise $800,000 for the reinforcement and restoration of the 130-year-old church, and also for construction of a parish hall. The campaign ended successfully, surpassing its initial goal.

The church building had been declared a historic landmark several years before; it was imperative to save the church from demolition by reinforcing the building to comply with new building codes and legislation. The parish council asked Mahoney to assess different possibilities with regard to raising funds, based on the feelings of the parishioners and the community. Once the results were tabulated and communicated, strategies to deal with effective communications, viable financial options to obtain donations, and realistic timetables were developed. Father O'Toole was in charge of dealing with all aspects of the construction as well as the capital campaign. O'Toole and Mahoney, in turn, directed a group of parishioners (the "leaders of the campaign") and worked closely with local community leaders.

The founding stories told by O'Toole and Mahoney, and other short-term partnerships with which we are familiar, all speak to several central issues in the formation and life of short-term partnerships. They all refer to the strong hopes of the partners that somehow the partnership they are forming will be different from most other business relationships. Typically, they assume or at least hope that their short-term partnership will be more innovative, more spontaneous, more trusting, and more gratifying than most long-term relationships.

During the initial "courtship" phase of short-term partnerships, many promises typically are made about hard work, commitment, and mutual appreciation. Frequently, short-term partnerships never move beyond this courtship phase. This is both a strength and a challenge for partners in short-term ventures. It is a problem because partners often do not give the partnership sufficient attention and often are unrealistic about the depth of commitment engendered by this type of partnership. As is the case in passionate but short-lived affairs of the heart, temporary partnerships may leave one partner feeling betrayed and isolated.

Both parties in a temporary partnership must be clear regarding their expectations, the duration and extent of the partnership, and the ways in which the partnership will be brought to a close. They should also realize that termination is likely to be accompanied by a grieving process, for if the partnership has been exciting it is likely to be enthralling and representative of the way in which both partners would like all of their business dealings to be.

The partners must realize that this level of trust and intensity cannot always be realized in a long-term relationship. The partnership often will "burn out" if it is designed for a sprint but later becomes a long-term marathon. The kind of changes that were described in earlier sections of this chapter will often be needed if a successful transition from short-term to long-term partnership is to take place. These changes may include shifts in governance, roles, responsibilities, communication patterns, and even ownership. It is particularly important that any shift in expectations regarding the duration and nature of a partnership be clearly articulated and that all partners be given ample opportunity to discuss the implications of these changes.

Partnerships That Don't Work and Have Been Brought to an End

Partnerships often go through difficult transitions; in some instances these actually lead to the demise of the partnership. This certainly seems to have been the case with Carol and Laura, whose research firms formed a partnership for about a decade as the Edgewood Research Group. A number of market-related factors began to make the original mission and role arrangements uncomfortable for Laura, Carol, and other members of both firms. Clients that Laura developed independently began to request services that were more oriented toward her staff's particular areas of research expertise.

This work was very interesting to Laura and the other members of her research staff, though it lay outside the mission of the Edgewood Research Group. Furthermore, Laura's original role as the partnership's primary "new venture" person fit less and less with what Laura did on a daily basis: marketing, sales presentations, and project management. While Edgewood was becoming more successful, Laura was finding that the market the partnership focused on was too constricting and that she had insufficient time to do R&D, which would enable them to expand their market and their services. She also was finding less and less time to initiate new ventures for her own firm.

Furthermore, as Edgewood became more successful, it also became more financially complex (as seems to be the case with many successful partnerships). The more powerful role that Carol originally took because of her credit line and highly competent administrative staff became increasingly inappropriate in a partnership where financial security was the result of the joint efforts of both firms. Laura attempted to raise these issues for discussion with Carol. It was at this point that the lack of an initial, explicit agreement regarding roles and responsibilities became painfully apparent. There were no agreements with regard to the maintenance of the partnership. There were no documents or partnership agreements on which to base a conversation.

The partnership and the two individual firms had become very busy. The initial, close working relationship between Laura and Carol had deteriorated, as their schedules allowed for less and less time together. They had developed no process for dealing with conflict. This case study certainly suggests that an initial formal agreement is often valuable, especially if the partners become very busy at a later point in the partnership or changes in the external environment suddenly require clarity of roles and responsibilities.

In this environment, Laura's attempts to discuss change were perceived as threatening by Carol. She had no interest in the research projects being conducted by Laura's firm, she had plenty of time for her own independent ventures, and she was quite happy with the progress Edgewood had made in its present market niche. Carol still saw herself as the majority contributor to the partnership, and she saw no reason to redefine roles. As Laura pushed the point, Carol suggested that Laura's firm try to make it on its own. Carol said that Laura's lack of "people skills" would sink her. She still saw Laura as she had in 1980, though it was now eight years later.

The inability to resolve the role conflict resulted in another change in the way the two firms worked together. Rather than making business decisions together, both Laura and Carol now avoided making any joint decisions. Each firm did what it wanted to do without checking with the other. Differentiation of functions and services reigned supreme, and integration of functions was abandoned. When certain actions later became known to members of the other firm, arguments would result. It is interesting to note that the superb talents of the research staff in both firms, along with a very strong market for the services the firms offered (separately and jointly), allowed Edgewood to continue to succeed for several more years, even though the partnership was dysfunctional at its core.

Laura and Carol developed a variety of coping mechanisms. They arranged schedules so that they were rarely in town at the same time. They hired a manager for their partnership venture who had the maturity to keep the peace by managing both of them. On two occasions, Laura attempted a more significant resolution by hiring an organization development consultant to help resolve the issues. Carol indicated that she could not work with either of these consultants. Edgewood limped through 1988 to 1991 in this fashion.

These coping mechanisms seemed to have worked successfully as long as the marketplace remained stable. However, the pathology of this partnership was rapidly exposed once there was a change in the market. As a result of the recession, several of Edgewood's largest clients began to downsize and to scale back their investments in basic research. As revenues began to drop, Edgewood could no longer afford to pursue a fragmented strategy. The need to clarify its mission was on the table again, now with a sense of urgency. Unfortunately, the partners could not constructively deal with the conflict.

Early in 1992, the partnership between Carol's and Laura's firms ended. Both of these very talented partners continue to own and run their own research firms, and both are doing well. At the time of the interview, Laura was still discovering Carol's acts of sabotage from when the partnership was dissolved four months earlier. Perhaps, had Carol been interviewed, she might also have interpreted some of Laura's acts as sabotage—a sad and painful end to a once-successful partnership and friendship.

What can be done in a case like this? How might the partnership have been reformed before it reached a stage where the only option was dissolution? How might the termination itself, if it was necessary, have been conducted in a more effective manner? First, we suggest that a key symptom of a partnership in trouble is a decline in direct communication between the partners. This partnership might have benefited from either internal or external assistance in opening lines of communication between the partners. Perhaps Laura (or Carol) should have continued to search for a consultant that both partners would have found acceptable. As is the case in marriages that are in trouble, a third party can often help the partners hear each other better, as well as serve as referee to ensure that the conversation does not simply become a means for one or both parties to hurt each other emotionally.

Second, this partnership could have benefited from clarification of roles and responsibilities. Once again, an external agent is often helpful in this regard. Such a person need not be a paid consultant or mediator. Often (especially in the case of a small business) the partners can identify a friend or colleague who is willing to listen to the stories of both partners and bring them together for a little trust-building and problem-solving.

Third, the partners need to be "given permission" to grieve for the loss of the relationship that once existed. Ironically, partners often cannot improve their relationship or bring the relationship to an end because they are too angry or too hurt to try either a reconciliation or a formal termination. Beneath this anger and hurt feelings are sorrow and a sense of loss. Both parties are likely to have experienced these feelings, and even when the partnership is terminated the partners should be encouraged to at least acknowledge these feelings and convey them to one another. Once again, a third party is often very helpful in this regard.

Finally, whether or not the partnership is terminated, the partners typically will need some expert assistance with regard to legal or business matters. Often a lawyer or business consultant can recommend an alternative governance structure, mode of decision-making, or business strategy that will help the partners get out of their current dilemma or terminate the partnership with minimal financial problems and legal hassles. This is no time to be "pound foolish." Poor decisions at this point can linger with the partners for many years to come.

Partnerships That Don't Work but Won't Be Brought to an End

Truth be known, partnerships (like marriages) sometimes—perhaps often—stay together simply because it's very hard to break apart. Several partners that we interviewed noted ethical, personal, legal, or financial reasons why they remain in their partnership. Despite many good reasons for breaking the partnership apart, such as continuing losses of money, incompatibility between the partners, loss of interest in the business, or the desire of one partner to move or retire, the partnership remains alive.

Sandra and Bill, for instance, have grown to dislike each other, yet the partnership between their companies (a medical supply house and a large pharmaceutical corporation) has remained intact. Clearly there have been several periods when their partnership has been in jeopardy. Each partner has wanted to leave at various times. However, the difficulties associated with leaving the partnership are what have kept it together.

According to Bill, the partnership stays together because both companies are good at what they do. They need each other in the rapidly changing world of medicine. Sandra's medical supply house, in particular, benefits greatly from Bill's pharmaceutical company. The partners' desire to dissolve the partnership centers on personal issues rather than work-related issues. The personal issues, in turn, have been resolved because Sandra and Bill feel that the partnership is important—and because the alternatives (going it alone or finding another partner) are unacceptable.

In some cases restraint stems from the partners' loyalty to the people they employ. While partnerships often thrive because of the close working relationship between their leaders and among their employees, these close relationships can also become a burden if the leaders want to discontinue the partnership or scale it back.

Partnerships often yield a very personal identification with the joint enterprise. People feel as if they are personally letting other people down if they move toward a "divorce." The impartiality and even anonymity that is a legal component of a corporation does not exist within a partnership. Partners are linked closely and personally to the welfare of the partnership, as well as its clients and employees. They can't simply pick up and leave. Thus partners must often learn how to work with and live through hard times—"for better or for worse."

One partnership we studied, between the medical service companies of Dr. Adams and Dr. Martin, provides a clear example of a partnership that should be terminated but continues to exist despite major headaches for all concerned. The case further illustrates what happens when a partnership has too much differentiation and not enough integration. As their partnership has become very large and complex, the partners' work has become increasingly isolated. Dr. Adams's company is responsible for most of the administrative services for both companies. His staff oversees sales, contract management, professional fee development, physician educational services, risk management, finance, accounting, physician enumeration, employee payroll, office operations, and other operational functions for both companies. Adams's company also independently manages seven ambulatory care centers. The organizational climate in the company is quite participatory and involving. Adams encourages personal and professional growth through education, and he highly encourages autonomous decision-making on the part of his staff. His staff works in a highly informal manner, and Adams frequently updates his staff on projects being conducted by the company. Discussion is encouraged and suggestions are welcomed.

Dr. Martin's company, by contrast, provides physician shift scheduling, recruitment, licensing, credentialing, and contract management for both companies. Like Dr. Adams's company, Dr. Martin has established an independent contract for his company to oversee several ambulatory care centers and to provide a variety of clinical services in other medical settings as well. Unlike Dr. Adams, Dr. Martin keeps a buffer between himself and his staff. He has only one department head reporting directly to him, and he prefers a traditional top-down, hierarchical structure. While Dr. Adams greets his employees when he enters the office, Dr. Martin tends to slip in the back door. His employees call him Dr. Martin, while Adams is addressed by his first name.

In this partnership we see a clear differentiation not only of functions, but also of management style and organizational culture. It is not unusual to see differences in style and culture accompany deep splits in a partnership. In this case the partners have virtually split the partnership in two and have maintained very few overlapping functions. There are no mechanisms of integration, perhaps because of the opposing views of Martin and Adams regarding the management of their own individual companies. The early years of the partnership proved to be the most effective, because the staff was smaller and the partnership required less integrative functions. There was open communication, and the business of medicine was less complex. The time of least effectiveness was about six years ago, during a period of very rapid expansion when there was a great need for integration (especially between the companies' sales staffs, who promised specific, partnership-based services, and the physicians, who had to provide the services).

The partnership formed by Adams and Martin has always been somewhat adversarial, and over the years their differences have grown even greater. Dr. Adams has gradually discontinued his clinical practice and focused solely on administrative functions, while Dr. Martin remains active clinically. The contributions Dr. Martin's company has made to the partnership have been primarily in the area of clinical backup to Dr. Adams's entrepreneurial endeavors. Martin and Adams rarely honor each other's distinctive contributions to the partnership, and they often complain about their partner's failures in the partnership. When asked if they would form this same partnership again, both partners answered with an emphatic no.

When a partnership needs to be dissolved because of profound incompatibility but there is major resistance—valid or not—to termination, then several steps can be taken. First, a formal mediator may be brought in to suggest ways in which the partnership can be terminated without undue damage to any party. There is rarely a partnership that can't be dissolved—this is one of the advantages of partnerships over more rigid corporate structures. The key is to obtain the services of a knowledgeable outside party who can identify and help evaluate the available options with a fresh and unbiased perspective.

Second, the partners often must confront their own "secondary gains" from the dysfunctional partnership. We previously identified one of these secondary gains when we described the "addiction" of many high tech partnerships to crisis. In addition, partners often remain in an ineffective partnership as a way of avoiding accountability for their own failure in their own organization—or in the partnership. Or they live out old personal conflicts through the partnership. Organizational and family "ghosts" from their personal life may haunt and distort the relationship between themselves and their partners. While this sounds like work for a psychotherapist, these issues can, in fact, be addressed without using an organizational "shrink." The partners must set aside a chunk of time to sit down together and talk candidly about what is going on in their strategic relationship.

Such candor can be sparked by having a third party ask each partner to identify at least one benefit he or she derives from the partnership's being "screwed up." The partners are likely to balk initially at this unusual request. However, the third party can come to the meeting prepared with several examples they have personally observed in the partnership. For example, one dysfunctional partnership we know gives each partner something to complain about virtually every day; this, in turn, enables members of one partner's executive staff to entertain themselves and their cohorts with many tales that divert attention away from other problems inside their own organization: "If we weren't in partnership with so-and-so, we would be a lot more successful." This convenient fiction, rarely challenged within the internecine confines of the partnership, hides many other problems in the organization—problems that would require personal sacrifice to correct, or a level of competence the complainant is not confident he or she possesses.

Finally, a "zombie partnership" that refuses to die often needs a self-imposed crisis in order to come to an end. One or more partners may need to elevate the stakes or make a unilateral decision that brings the issue of termination to a head. One partner, for instance, may threaten to unilaterally withdraw from the partnership within one or two months. Or one participating organization may indicate that it will no longer be actively involved in the partnership after a certain period of time. While such actions may seem extreme, they often are needed in order to bring a humane end to a relationship that is no longer either constructive or productive. The pain associated with termination is typically no worse than the ongoing pain associated with a dysfunctional partnership. One must choose between two evils: termination is painful for a relatively short period of time; staying in a bad situation can be painful for a very long period of time.

The Essential Points

1. Effective transitions in partnerships require acceptance of (even enthusiasm for) the processes of change, acknowledgement of the need for continuity, and broad-based support for the partnership and its sustaining vision.

2. When a transition in either membership or leadership occurs, a partnership is likely to go through a period of major stress and potential dissolution. Partnerships, in this sense, are more vulnerable to change than are traditional, hierarchical organizations.

3. Frequently partnerships bring on their own crises and needs for change and transitions in form or function, often as a result of the partnership's own success and growth.

4. Partnerships are likely to be successful in today's turbulent business environment if they take advantage of their status as "open systems," which are particularly amenable to learning.

5. Partnerships are likely to be successful in responding to the shifting needs and demands of the contemporary marketplace if they take advantage of their status as product-, service-, or consumer-oriented relationships.

6. Some partnerships must be radically redesigned in order to remain viable, while others are intentionally designed to be

short-lived. Eventually most partnerships must be terminated, and partners should retain sufficient independence (financially and psychologically) to bring a partnership to an end before it becomes dysfunctional or destructive.

7. Unfortunately, some partnerships cannot readily be terminated, even though they are no longer functional and may even be destructive. The difficulties associated with terminating some partnerships speaks to the care that must be taken in establishing binding partnerships in the first place.

Part Three

Partnerships in Practice

Chapter Six

Lesher Communications and Norpac

A Supplier-Customer Partnership

In setting the context for the study of this partnership, we asked one of the central players in the drama to comment on the partnership's origins and initial purposes. This person, Don Jochens, serves as director of production at Lesher Communications, one of the two partners. According to Don, the story begins with the formation of a publishing company, Lesher Communications, by Dean Lesher during the 1940s. Lesher was a classic entrepreneur and rogue individualist; his name has taken on almost legendary proportions in the San Francisco area since his recent death. Lesher began by buying the *Green Sheet*, a small advertising publication that was located in the East Bay, east of the city, when the area was still mostly undeveloped, open land. He gradually bought up most of the local newspaper market by customizing the news and advertising content to the local readership. Today Lesher Communications dominates the East Bay newspaper business, achieving a market penetration that is 10 to 20 percent above industry standards. In addition, Lesher Communications prints the northern California editions of the *New York Times*.

On the other side of the alliance is the Weyerhaeuser Corporation, a large forest products corporation. In the late 1970s, George Weyerhaeuser, great-grandson of the founder of the giant paper and pulp supplier, approached the Jujo Paper Company, a paper manufacturer in Japan (now the Nippon Paper Company, the second largest in Japan). Together, the heads of these two companies spawned the mutually beneficial idea of opening a newsprint paper mill in the United States. The North Pacific Paper Corporation (Norpac), the product of this joint venture, provides Weyerhaeuser with the opportunity to benchmark their manufacturing processes against the high standards of Nippon's, while Nippon gets advantageous access to a long-term supply of paper. Half of Norpac's production is distributed in the United States, and half of it is sold to Japanese publishers.

Getting Started: Forming the Partnership

Jim Taylor, materials manager at Norpac, notes that Norpac is an exceptional joint venture, given that it was established between one of the largest U.S. forest products suppliers and one of Japan's largest paper mills. Nippon and Weyerhaeuser signed a joint venture agreement in 1976; they launched their new paper mill in Longview, Washington, as a privately held company under the name Norpac in 1979. Taylor notes that the alliance represented several new ventures for both giants. First, it meant a new plant for both companies, as well as a new product line for Weyerhaeuser. It was Weyerhaeuser's first joint venture with a Japanese company, and it was the first time either company had codesigned a product from scratch. The stage was thus set for an even more innovative venture—a partnership with Lesher Communications.

Because Norpac was itself a partnership, its leaders were quite open to further alliances. Norpac had already established less formal partnerships with ten suppliers prior to its partnership with Lesher. While Lesher was Norpac's first partnership with a customer, Norpac, according to Taylor, was still able to use its partnering experience in setting up this special relationship: "Each [of our existing partnerships] has varying levels of involvement, depending on several factors: impact on the quality of our product, impact on the performance of our people, changeability of requirements, and the amount of communication needed for the relationship to work. Many of our supply partners approached us, and we are currently reviewing how many we can realistically sustain. They take a lot of work. The relationship grows side by side with the business agreement."

The alliance between Lesher and Norpac grew out of tough economic times in the newspaper industry. Lesher had to maintain almost a two-month paper supply (worth millions in capital) because of the unsure nature of their supplier relationships and because a reliable paper supply is of central importance to its business. It is common practice for newspaper publishers to have three to five newsprint suppliers, to guard against having their newsprint cut off or being at the mercy of vendors with regard to cost. According to Don Jochens, Lesher's director of production, "The mind-set was that no matter how much you bought from a supplier you had to control them, or you wouldn't be able to control supply or cost."

Then the tables turned. The newspaper industry experienced a glut of paper on the market. Many paper manufacturers were adding new mills, and as a result of the increased supply, prices started to drop. Because they produce a superior-quality paper that is in great demand, Norpac was unwilling to come down in price as much as some other suppliers. As a result, Lesher removed Norpac from its supply chain. "We had three other mills we were using at the time," Jochens explains, "and although their prices were lower, we had problems with all three—problems with delivery and quality of the paper. Although we were trying to gain control with multiple suppliers, in the end we really had very little control."

In 1992 Lesher's press manager, Sam Foster, and Craig Guernsey, a Weyerhaeuser newsprint sales manager, discussed the prospect of working together in a single-source relationship. The problems of poor quality and unreliable delivery were ones Lesher had not experienced with Norpac. Jochens recalls:

We both expressed an interest in opening a partnership agreement and, as a result, the quality of our relationship with them enabled us to run our operations much more smoothly. . . . In a paradoxical way, we began to realize that maybe control has more to do with controlling the quality of our operation, and therefore the quality of our own product, than it has to do with manipulating multiple vendor relationships. We were spending an incredible amount of time and energy trying to control our supply, and in the end, we had wasted time and energy and had nothing but frustration to show for it.

Interviews with Nancy Maher and Marty Begall, leaders of Lesher's new high-tech, worker-run Concord plant, revealed more about the founding of the partnership. According to Maher, "As we pursued our alliance we became more aware of the benefits of partnering with Norpac. Basically our agreement was that we were wiling to guarantee our business in exchange for a price they were giving to their largest-volume customers, who bought volumes equal to or greater than our total usage." Maher and Begall also discovered that Lesher shared a common organizational culture and set of beliefs with Norpac about how to run operations and involve employees in the decision-making processes of the company. Both organizations were working with high-involvement management strategies—what are often called sociotechnical systems—self-managing teams, and the like (see Lawler, 1986, 1992). Maher suggests that the leaders at Lesher "realized that the synergies in the way Lesher and Norpac do business would make for a deeper, even more powerful relationship than we initially imagined. The whole thing just blossomed!"

As Nancy Maher observed, Norpac is committed, like Lesher, to high levels of employee involvement. As Taylor puts it, "We share information about how we're doing in our business. Every crew has monthly business meetings, and salaried people have quarterly meetings to look at overall company performance. We've gone through a renewal process, redefining our direction and management practices." Norpac's current management objectives include developing teams capable of even higher performance. Taylor believes that "there is a lot more capacity across our work force for teams to take on more responsibility for their own performance, for working out their relationship issues within the team . . . to confront one another on team performance, and put more emphasis on decision making at all levels."

Taylor indicates that Norpac's attitudes about involvement are carried over into its customer relationships. According to Taylor, Norpac is a desirable partner because "we have a lot of pride at being the best. We've developed a reputation in the U.S. market as being the top-quality producer of newsprint. We are also recognized for our service. We go out of our way to serve our customers." Furthermore, everyone at Norpac works closely with each of Norpac's customers. Employees do not just focus on a single customer, but also gain firsthand knowledge of the operations in each of their customer's organization. For example, 40 percent of Norpac's customer-based production is in Japan. Thirty percent of Norpac's five hundred employees have traveled to Japan to visit many of these customer sites.

Both Taylor and Maher seem to be suggesting that partnerships thrive not only when both organizations share certain common values, but also when these values include a shared commitment to broad-based participation in product design and decision-making processes, as well as high product quality. The common vision adopted by these two companies clearly articulates this shared commitment: "A long-term, mutually beneficial relationship that is based upon open communication and trust with a common goal of continuous improvement. It will be people-driven with linkages at all levels for better understanding of common expectations."

Structuring the Partnership

In July 1992 Lesher put together a formal, but very loose, contract with Norpac that basically restated their verbal agreements plus added a few other clauses. Both parties signed it, and the partnership was officially launched. To kick off the partnership, George

Riggs, president of Lesher Communications, and Don Jochens flew up to Longview, Washington, about fifty miles north of Portland, where Norpac is headquartered. They met with a group of Norpac's executives and people from Weyerhaeuser. Riggs and Jochens, along with the executives from Norpac and Weyerhaeuser, spent a day brainstorming what they wanted to do with the partnership. They formed two committees: the "sponsor group" included the mill manager from Norpac, the vice president of sales and marketing from Weyerhaeuser, and George Riggs, Lesher's president; the "steering committee" consisted of five people from Lesher, including Jochens, Sam Foster (press manager), and Foster's night supervisor, and two people from the new worker-run Concord Plant—Nancy Maher, the plant manager, and Marty Begall, one of the press people.

According to Begall, the initial meetings of the steering committee were filled with apprehension—at least on his part. His attitude soon changed, however, and he saw many immediate benefits:

> I went into [the steering committee] fairly confused about what to expect out of it. What I've seen . . . for the most part is . . . understanding and trust. A lot of trust. In the past, newsprint suppliers . . . would stop by once in a while, watch a run, shake their heads, and leave. They added little or no value. It was merely a transaction. People from Norpac aren't like that. These people give you some answers. Their paper is top quality, and they respond immediately to something and at least have some information for you. We hardly have to make any trouble calls. They are on top of their business with us.

One of the first problems the steering committee faced was with "curl." Curl—an industrywide problem—occurs when the outside edge of the paper coming through a press curls up. This can create many different problems for the press operator, because the paper either folds over or the finished product curls up at the corner. Begall notes that "Norpac was aware of the problem right at the time we started the partnership. We constantly talked to them, and they said they were working on the problem. They were working to solve the problem. And they did. It only took a short period of time before the problem was resolved, and I think that with other manufacturers they wouldn't have been so readily able to respond so quickly." Begall observed that "most companies would have written the problem off as a bad batch of paper. Instead, we shared information from both sides to help analyze it and eventually worked through it together to understand the whole picture." Now Lesher and Norpac are working together as a single problem-solving team on this difficult problem.

The steering committee meets monthly, rotating locations. As a result, members of the committee have spent time at each site, learning about each other's business. They've taken tours, spent some time in each of the major operations areas, shared a lot of information about the structure of the two organizations as well as some confidential information about operations. Norpac even shared information about how well they were doing in the recession with price cuts and everything else. Jochens notes, "Basically we have treated each other as insiders. There was a lot of sharing of some very confidential information, and it helped build a lot of trust."

In January 1993 the steering committee finally had enough things resolved that it only needed to meet quarterly thereafter. Quarterly steering committee meetings are held at Norpac, with all the employees. According to Will Walters, technical services manager for domestic markets at Norpac, these quarterly meetings, both internally and cross-company, are needed to ensure high-quality service to customers geographically dispersed across 130 locations. Recently Walters asked the Lesher members of the joint steering committee to begin attending his quarterly internal staff meetings so Norpac could be briefed on performance of their newsprint at Lesher's production sites. Jochens thought it was such a great idea that he has begun the same sort of internal and cross-reporting meetings with his employees at Lesher. Jochens indicates that "we've begun to incorporate expanded standards into our reporting now. We want to talk about our productivity, our on-time performance, our quality, our impact on the environment, safety issues, social issues, and team development relative to the standards we've set. I've been amazed at the degree of improvement in our performance. These meetings have been very effective and helpful in sharing information about our performance with all of our employees."

Lesher and Norpac launched a cooperative training program in which employees from both businesses learn by working on-site at each others' operations. Every five weeks Lesher sends two people to Longview, Washington, for a week of milling paper, and two Norpac employees go to Walnut Creek and Concord. Lesher provides full on-the-job training for these Norpac visitors, in which they have the experience of running the paper produced in their mill.

These experiences make both Lesher and Norpac employees feel like business partners, deep into both organizations. Walters suggests that Norpac's and Lesher's employees benefit greatly from the cross-training: "We each send our employees to each other's sites for a week each month, and as a result, we have a much bigger picture of how our business works from the point of view of our customers. That firsthand perspective is invaluable."

The benefits for both Lesher and Norpac don't stop there. Although Lesher is one of only a few customer partnerships, Norpac has entered into many partnership relationships with its vendors. One of those is with Interstate Distributors, a trucking company. The relationship between Norpac and Interstate has benefited Lesher as well. The long trailer-trucks used to ship paper often leak. In winter their tires kick up snow, which is thrown up into the truck. To keep the paper dry, the truckers line their trucks with plastic as a temporary solution. After several deliveries, the plastic is chewed up and can't readily be recycled.

Through their steering committee, Lesher and Norpac began working on the problem and came up with a different approach. Lesher worked jointly with the trucking company, putting together diagrams of the way they load certain trucks in their fleet to determine where the water infiltration was occurring. Now the trucking company uses cardboard, which is recyclable, and has begun loading the paper in a way that tends to avoid water damage. These alternative solutions cost much less and make use of more environmentally friendly materials.

"This kind of resolution," according to Begall, "would not have happened without the three of us working together as partners. Just [having] the freedom to pick up the phone and say, 'Hey, we're having a problem, can you help us?' and know that the response will be positive—that is worth everything." Begall and other Lesher employees can now call the truckers directly: "We all work very closely together. Two years ago we would have just switched suppliers. . . . That would only be a temporary solution."

Clearly, one successful partnership seems to beget other partnerships. Jochens and Foster mentioned that Lesher has already signed a single-source agreement with an ink manufacturer. Apparently one of the major problems facing Lesher at the present time is the disposal of ink waste, especially when it's toxic. The ink Lesher uses is petroleum-based. As a result, Foster notes, "The only thing [we] could do when we were finished with it was to take it to the landfill. We feel that we should assume responsibility for our waste, and [we need] to change these practices. We began recycling ink in our own plant. We have worn out our reclaiming unit, so our ink supplier has offered to purchase a new reclaiming unit in exchange for an exclusive contract for five years. In exchange, we want to have something to say about the quality of their ink."

Lesher could potentially save more than a million dollars by collaborating with its ink supplier. It costs $700 per drum to send waste ink out to a landfill and buy new ink. Lesher uses one to four barrels of ink per week. Foster enthusiastically notes that "the savings will be fantastic"—it's a lovely blend of environmental consciousness and financial benefit. In reflecting on the newly emerging Lesher partnerships, Foster suggests that "the key in all of this is the trust and willingness to collaborate on getting the best final product, and doing it with a view of all the quality issues. No one has an edge on anyone else. We are just joining forces for the mutual benefit of the whole, with a wide-angle lens."

Before the partnership with Norpac, there was a big garbage dumpster sitting outside Lesher's Walnut Creek office. Lesher used to pay $500 for a load of garbage to be hauled away. When Lesher and Norpac created their partnership, Norpac began to provide this service. They didn't charge Lesher for it, but they would take the dumpster back to the recycling plant. Now Lesher employees separate the garbage before putting it in the dumpster, and Norpac pays Lesher for the paper they take to their recycling division, which supplies pulp for their paper machine. In fact, Norpac now takes care of all of Lesher's newsprint waste. According to Jochens, "They take our wrappers back and recycle them. We couldn't recycle part of the wrapper because it had glue on it. You can't recycle the glue. So we came up with a wax that now they put on the ends, and it works as well as the glue and now we can recycle these. These are the bales that we send back up. They take all of our cardboard back."

Jochens describes the Lesher-Norpac partnership as a circle: "They ship us paper. We use it, make waste out of it, give it right back to them, and it just keeps going around. The paper that you see here could have been paper that we purchased from the mill last month." Jochens notes that the same type of circle is now in place between Lesher and Interstate Trucking: "The truckers used to deliver their load and just sit around waiting while we unloaded the goods. Now the driver backs in and inspects the sheets for damage and records the information. So we've cut our labor cost in half because the trucker is doing one of 'our' jobs. Well, I don't know if you've ever worked with truckers, but [their] doing extra work is pretty unusual."

The potential is great—perhaps unlimited—for this growing series of partnerships. Begall envisions multiple alliances strung together as if they were operating as a single business. In this way the members of these partnerships create a vertical integration of services and products. The partners serve each other, adding value up the supply chain to the end user.

Managing and Expanding the Partnership

Norpac has a formal continuous-improvement program that concerns managing information and product flow. The steering committee members from Lesher saw this program in operation and liked it. Norpac has offered to send trainers to work with Lesher at no cost. As Lesher becomes even more skillful at implementing their own quality-improvement efforts, they will be able to more effectively share information with Norpac about its newsprint. As we noted above, frequent sharing of information seems to be a central ingredient in successful partnerships. The open communication channels, in turn, help Norpac provide a better product to all of their customers. For instance, Norpac will become even more fully involved in Lesher's research and development efforts with the ink supplier, thereby helping Norpac do a better job of producing newsprint that is fully compatible with the new inks being created. This joint venture should benefit Norpac as well as Lesher in the improvement of quality and reduction of costs.

Craig Guernsey, from Weyerhaeuser's sales department, says bluntly, "Our relationship with Lesher is pretty much a one-sided venture." He believes that the arrangement at this point favors Lesher. However, the partnership with Lesher has helped Weyerhaeuser experiment with newsprint, and Weyerhaeuser employees are learning, firsthand, how one of their customers works and thinks. "Eventually," Guernsey explains, "we feel that 'thinking like the customer' will give us a competitive advantage." Although much of the value of the relationship is for Lesher right now, the participating employees at Weyerhaeuser believe that their increased knowledge of their customers will become an advantage in anticipating new products, new specifications, new services, and so forth. This is a long-term commitment.

Weyerhaeuser has recently entered into a similar venture with another of its customers. Guernsey notes that "it's a lot of work on the front end defining and structuring the agreement . . . [and] spending time together. As a result, we want to be selective about who we partner with. We think [Lesher] is a good fit. Our culture and team orientation is similar, the volume they provide is reasonable, and it will strengthen our positioning in the marketplace."

Vonnie Moore, a Weyerhaeuser newsprint-sales services manager who works with Lesher in the areas of service and logistics, offers a similar perspective regarding the characteristics that make Lesher different from most of Weyerhaeuser's other customers and potential partners. Moore believes that the key characteristic is trustworthiness. The relationship provides a broad base for sharing information about the financial performance and changes in both corporations. Moore suggests that "we are probably both more open-minded with each other, willing to try new things and solve problems together. We have better feedback and communication . . . [that is] more timely and specific. We are developing a common understanding of each other's operations."

Moore still wonders, however, about how open Weyerhaeuser and Lesher can be with each other about pricing and costs of their respective services. The extent of this openness between vendor and customer will be a real test. To what degree should customer cost structures affect Weyerhaeuser's pricing, or vice versa? To what degree should a customer's increased margins and/or savings allow a company like Weyerhaeuser to increase its price on goods and services to this customer? Where will cooperative pricing and costing have to end?

These difficult questions are clearly very important and must be addressed by Weyerhaeuser, Lesher, Norpac, and virtually every other business involved in communications and publishing. Clearly the mass-communication business is changing. Newspaper companies like Lesher Communications have to think differently as an industry if they are going to survive. Lesher's business is expanding, but unfortunately the increased volume is in areas where it costs more to produce, and they are losing business in areas with less overhead. For example, if Lesher loses one page of classified advertising, it takes two to three large display ads to generate the same revenue. And added to this problem is the expansion of giant discounters like Wal-Mart, Food 4 Less, and Price Costco: these companies don't advertise; they don't need to, because everyone knows their reputation for low prices.

Sam Foster concludes that "our industry is going to die one day, unless newspapers and all their vendors—ink plates, newsprint, chemicals—get into some kind of partnership. There is a shift in advertising. You can buy localized advertising on . . . TV for broadcast within a community. Smaller businesses can advertise by direct mail. We can potentially lose a lot of advertisement if we don't change, too. Interactive [partnerships] may even redefine advertising as we know it."

Lesher's relationship with Norpac has been enlightening for everyone connected with Lesher, including Lesher's other partners. Members of the steering committee have accomplished much just by sitting down to talk about their shared needs and problems. Jochens suggests that "eventually we need to build that kind of relationship with all of our key suppliers to win in this game. We are all a part of each other's business."

Sustaining the Partnership

The partnership between Lesher and Norpac is producing results. Information is being communicated among a broader base of people, and as a result, change is rippling through both organizations. When Lesher had three or four suppliers, the company kept between sixty and ninety days' worth of newsprint on hand. A roll of newsprint weighs about three-quarters of a ton. A ton of newsprint runs about $600. Lesher goes through about seventy rolls a day. As a result, Lesher had several million dollars tied up in newsprint. According to Jochens, "In the first five months we've been working together we . . . cut our inventory down to about ten days', down from seventy days'. That's a seven hundred percent reduction, and we're still working to reduce it further! Now we have a couple of hundred thousand dollars' [worth] of inventory sitting on our floor rather than a couple of million."

Because of a reduced need to keep a large supply of newsprint on hand, Lesher has been able to cut the floor space used for newsprint inventory by half. Their warehouse can hold up to thirty days' supply of newsprint. Lesher used to pay for extra storage space in San Jose. Now that Norpac guarantees a supply, Lesher is using its newly freed warehouse space to build an exercise room for its employees.

As a representative of Norpac, Will Walters also speaks with pride about the benefits that this partnership has brought to Lesher in terms of reduced warehousing costs: "Lesher was our first customer partnership. We have contractual agreements on a few important things. Our commitment is to always be competitive with price and quality. We have also agreed to ensure that Lesher always has a supply of paper. As a result, they have reduced the need to warehouse their own paper supply and have returned three million dollars to their bottom line."

The second major benefit to Lesher concerns a reduction in paper waste. When one roll of paper is just about at an end, a press operator must push a "paster" sheet against the expiring roll of paper at exactly the right moment to begin the new roll and sever the old roll. The goal is to save paper and to start the new roll without a break in the run. When Lesher had multiple suppliers, and therefore used multiple types of paper, the result was about an inch of paper left on each core. With paper costing $600 a ton, this represented a major expense. As a result of its single-source relationship with Norpac, Lesher has reduced its paper waste to one-eighth inch per roll. This one improvement has provided a substantial savings.

Another savings has resulted from decreasing the occurrence of "web" breaks, which happen when paper disengages from the press. When the paper disengages the press stops, and the press operators must "web" the paper back onto the press. This repair is very costly. In the past Lesher had a break every thirty to forty rolls. Using high-quality Norpac paper, they now average more than eighty rolls between breaks. In the first nine months of its partnership, Lesher significantly reduced its newsprint waste.

What are the benefits that accrue to Norpac under this partnership agreement? Several of the benefits are obvious. Norpac is assured of a major customer it does not have to compete for. The agreement with Lesher guarantees business in excess of twenty thousand tons of paper annually. Several other benefits, although less obvious, are of great value to Norpac's ability to stay ahead of its competition. Walters notes that Norpac now has access to the Lesher pressroom in order to test Norpac products. As a result, Norpac now gets much more accurate information about the performance of its paper.

Previously, Norpac had to rely on unsystematic and usually critical feedback from its customers. When things were going well they would hear nothing; and when they received negative feedback, Norpac could never be certain that its paper was at fault. They suspected—and Lesher employees confirmed—that frequently the newsprint was blamed for mistakes that actually had been made by press operators. It is always easier to blame an outside supplier than to look for an internal culprit. Now, with the open sharing of information between Norpac and Lesher, Norpac employees receive a much less biased assessment of their product and can test it themselves in actual use. Because of their experience with Lesher, Norpac employees are learning to think like their customers.

A final benefit seems to apply to both partners. This benefit concerns what Nancy Maher from Lesher calls the "cultural synergy" that has been established between these two innovative companies. Maher makes this observation:

Our Concord plant began its operations in 1990 with a very different operating philosophy than exists in the main operation in Walnut Creek. At the time we were not using Norpac. We were brought in a little later. . . . At Concord, we had a particular interest in joining with Norpac because our cultures were very similar. Our plant was organized and staffed on a sociotechnical, team-based operating philosophy. Norpac's operations ran on a similar ideology. We believed that a business partnership would be even more powerful because of our similar beliefs about empowering people. There is a cultural synergy that has made a good marriage. We have built on each other's strengths.

In the field of publishing, as in many process-oriented businesses, there is a chain of relationships between a number of different businesses. Pulp, paper manufacturing, transportation, ink, and publishing all make a difference regarding the quality of the final product, the published newspaper. Neither Lesher nor Norpac could achieve this overall quality on its own. They need each other if either company is to compete in a rapidly changing and technologically demanding marketplace. Typically, even with the interdependency of the various businesses along the chain, each business operates independently and often in an adversarial or at least very guarded relationship with each other. In the case of Lesher and Norpac, however, the traditional relationship has been transformed into a partnership that, in turn, allows both companies to be more effective in responding to volatile economic conditions.

"I have this picture," confides Jochens, "of taking the complete chain of activities, from the very beginning to the very end, and [putting] everybody involved together, working side by side. Everybody could have a look at each . . . set of activities, like the truckers and the timber people and the advertisers, and everybody could see the whole. . . . It would probably be incredible in terms of the ease with which the whole product could be conceived, manufactured, and distributed." Jochens notes that in the printing industry it's common for suppliers to wine and dine their customers. However, according to Jochens, "when Norpac comes into town, we take them out. We make sure they don't spend any money while they're here. It's breaking the traditional mind-set of suppliers and customers."

Weyerhaeuser—one of the two partners in Norpac—is a very large corporation, and Lesher is one of its smaller customers. Yet Weyerhaeuser seems to be very concerned about what is happening at Lesher. Nancy Maher indicates that they really treat Lesher like a major customer. According to Maher, "At this point, they are better able to serve us than we are to serve them. If there is a problem we call them up. There is never a problem getting a hold of somebody. We don't have the staffing and are not able to reciprocate as well as they do. I guess I feel almost overwhelmed. We are learning from them. And we share information with them, so I guess they are learning from us. I wonder what we are doing for them other than being open and honest with them."

It's hard to imagine, until recently, that we might hear about a customer concerned that they are getting more than they are giving to their supplier. In true partnerships, however, service takes on a higher meaning. If we can all serve the whole, the parts reap the benefits, too.

In commenting on what sustains the partnership between Lesher and Norpac, Don Jochens of Lesher says that the men and women of Norpac are as excited about these outcomes as the Lesher employees are—given that they have contributed to the success of one of their customers, they can point with pride to this accomplishment when meeting with other potential customers. Finally, the end user is the real beneficiary of this partnership: a daily newspaper is delivered on time with the clarity of color and print that makes the news easier to read and the ads more appealing. Jochens observes that "media buyers love our paper. We think the people in our community do, too. The value to them is intrinsic to the quality of what we all do." Behind Jochens's comments about the enduring quality of the Lesher-Norpac partnership lies a shared vision: empowered work forces, trust, a mutual commitment to work things out, and a dedication to quality.

Chapter Seven

Arthur Andersen and the Alameda School System

A Public-Private Collaboration

Like many good partnerships, the joint venture between Arthur Andersen, a global accounting firm, and the Alameda, California, school system wasn't formed as a conscious, planned event. Arthur Andersen started working with Alameda in the spring of 1991, out of the firm's deep and long-term commitment to education. Nancy Clark was recently named director of Andersen's School of the Future, Western Region. She recalls the school's start-up:

> Our firmwide effort started shortly after the release of *A Nation at Risk*. In 1985, Arthur Andersen got involved in public education as a result of a strategic planning project with the city of Detroit. By going through a visioning and planning process with the Detroit community, it became clear that the city was experiencing many difficult problems, not unlike many [other] cities. As we worked to understand the causes of these problems, we found ourselves "upstream" examining the education system. For us, the strategic planning project for Detroit underscored that we were indeed a nation at risk. More important, it led us to the understanding that education was not the problem but the solution. If we were to make systemic improvement in our communities, our school systems would need to be one of the key leaders of that reform.

As a result of Arthur Andersen's work with the city of Detroit, Dick Measelle (who was then the managing partner at the Detroit office and subsequently became the managing partner for Arthur

Andersen) convened a meeting of some of Arthur Andersen's best strategic thinkers. Being a visionary, as well as a civic-minded person, Measelle challenged the firm's leaders to discover ways Arthur Andersen could help public education. According to Nancy Clark, Measelle said, "We pride ourselves on helping business organizations change and anticipate the future, we are leading experts in finance and systems, and we run the premier professional education center in the world. We train over forty-five thousand people a year. Surely, there must be something that we can do to support public education."

Arthur Andersen has a 145-acre, fully staffed education center in St. Charles, Illinois, with 150 M.A.'s and 30 Ph.D.'s who work exclusively to design, develop, implement, and assess education courses for partners and employees. With this considerable resource behind them, members of the firm spent two years trying to identify some of the key issues facing contemporary school systems. Team members in St. Charles asked many questions about the K–12 system which brought them closer to addressing the core problems facing many school systems and their communities:

- What are the causes of the school systems' declining ability to prepare kids in the basics and inspire them to pursue continuing education?

- Why is the school system the holding pen for all of the community's ills?

- Why has the education system remained the same since the days of Horace Mann—the 1890s—while the workplace it feeds has changed dramatically?

- How can the complex and rapidly increasing demands being placed on the schools by society and the workplace be met?

- How do we reinvent education, in the face of a declining economy, over the next twenty, thirty, or forty years?

Clark suggests that "answers for these questions require quantum leaps in how we think about education. Most change at this level is discontinuous. You can increase the speed of a car exponentially and it will never leave the ground in flight." Insights generated from these staff discussions were distributed throughout Arthur Andersen. There was a prevailing concern within the firm that, as a business, Arthur Andersen was beginning to focus on K–12 while its primary business relied on hiring and grooming college graduates. They were concerned about moving further away from their source of new recruits. Others in the firm realized that if Arthur Andersen were going to expect a pool of high-caliber college graduates each year, the company had to look upstream into the whole system, from prekindergarten to postgraduate education.

Just looking at the statistics alone is cause for considering a partnership between business and education. Clark noted that, on average, there is a 30 percent dropout rate at the high school level. In some inner city schools it is as high as 70 or 80 percent. Colleges experience a 50 percent dropout rate. If, in addition, there is a decline in the competency of the students who remain, the supply of qualified graduates is diminishing substantially. "These statistics are not an immediate concern," according to Clark, but "they are ultimately a big concern if business is going to share . . . ownership for educating its work force."

Getting Started: Formation of the Partnership

Through a series of events, Arthur Andersen's San Francisco office began to get more involved in public education, initially because several of its major clients were similarly involved. Sam Ginn, then CEO of Pacific Telesis, was one of those clients. He was a past president of the Industry Education Council, a conglomeration of business, labor, and education professionals concerned about education. One of Arthur Andersen's partners, Greg Conlon, was on the board at the time. He began to share some of the research coming out of St. Charles, which dovetailed with the concerns of the council. At the same time, Nancy Clark, who eventually became Arthur Andersen's most active player on this project, was going through some personal introspection that caused her to rethink her own values and her feelings about giving something back to society.

Concurrent with Arthur Andersen's local activity, the state of California passed legislation to provide funding to schools that wanted to rethink education—schools that wanted to do something radically different. With the encouragement of the Industry Education Council, Arthur Andersen began to look for a school district to form a partnership with. Clark suggests that Arthur Andersen chose the Alameda Unified School District (AUSD) because it possessed several key characteristics: it had "a leader who was open to forming a partnership, even though the partnership was ill defined; it was representative of the rich socioeconomic, ethnic, and age diversity resident in California; it was the right size; and it was urban."

John Searles, who was then superintendent of the AUSD, offers his own version of the first steps in structuring the partnership between his school system and Arthur Andersen:

> I sat on the board of the Industry Education Council with Greg Conlon. I really didn't know him very well. Joan Bowen is really the one who gets credit for bringing us together. She was the president of the council in 1991. She was big on involving industry in the schools. She felt that industry had a vested interest in the work force and that schools could use the resources and disciplines of business. She was also impressed with Greg Conlon. So she pushed hard to get us together and we finally gave in.
>
> In our first meetings I think we both discovered that Alameda was already considering and using some of the ideas that came out of Arthur Andersen's research at St. Charles. Things like cooperative learning, where kids work together to learn, and the concept of

developmental learning, where the child's education is tailored more to his or her own developmental stage rather than structured by grade. We were already doing some of this.

Searles went on to note that he was having difficulty with some of the Alameda school board members. Three of the five members didn't want to renew his contract; however, there was such an uprising from the community that they backed off and his contract was renewed for two years in March 1991. Several opportunities and problems were coming to a head. Searles felt that he had to act, and it was important to him that the school system "move forward rather than backward."

Structuring the Partnership

Arthur Andersen and the Alameda school district began by writing a grant request to the state of California. Arthur Andersen's staff quickly realized that they needed to partner with Alameda in a much deeper way. According to Clark, "We wanted to join them in rethinking the whole of education, and include the community." Nancy Clark indicated that when her firm began working with Alameda's schools to write the grant request, both partners began to think in new and different ways about the problems the school system was facing at the time. Michael Doyle, a consultant who had worked with Arthur Andersen in the Detroit project, began to work with the emerging venture between Arthur Andersen and Alameda, to engage the broader community in creating a vision for education. Over the course of the next year the partners recruited over twelve hundred students, parents, teachers, administrators, and businesspeople to rethink education in their community. They worked collaboratively in building the vision, values, and culture that are necessary for change in a community's education system.

Through this process, a broad constituency in Alameda began to see that the school district's focus, as it was currently operating, wasn't on learning. Rather it was on keeping a record of how many minutes a student was in class and whether or not the teachers could keep them quiet. These factors added no value to the educational process, but they were the basis for funding. Yet, as Clark noted, "we all know that when we're learning, we're active and engaged. This was really a systems issue that we needed to fix."

To carry out their vision of radical reform in the school system, strategic teams were formed by the partners. One of the teams was responsible for community support and marketing. Its primary purpose was to keep members of the community informed and involved. Other teams were responsible for curriculum development, staff assessment and development, and technology advancement. Site teams were also established to assist the individual schools in creating their own plans. Clark suggested that "the process was dynamic more than linear. Several basic building blocks are now being put in place that will serve as a platform for expanding our work." Clark added that the success of this process depended on the degree to which the community of Alameda and its school system developed ownership of the ongoing change effort. Documentation of the partners' vision and an accompanying profile of school system graduates would serve as a common reference as the individual school sites began to design their own changes. Once the individual school sites had built momentum, Clark adds, the central administration of the partnership developed a better sense of what they needed to offer.

Clark concluded that, in two years of working together, participants from both Arthur Andersen and the Alameda school system had all learned a lot about each other, "student to student, teacher to teacher, parent to teacher, and so on." As with the Lesher-Norpac partnership, one of the first and biggest challenges for both partners was building trust. This primarily occurred through reliance on frequent and open communication (the second vital ingredient in any partnership). Clark suggested that members of the Arthur Andersen group had to remember that they were working with

Alameda on *their* turf. The faculty and staff in Alameda are the experts about education and the needs of their community. Clark observed that "we were guests in *their* house, and although we might have suggestions [about] moving the furniture around, it would be rude to move it unless asked. We've had to learn *their* vocabulary, and work in *their* culture. Our contribution came from our respect for them and their role in our society, from our resourcefulness as external agents of change, *and* our role as team players."

For the first year, people in the school district were sure that Arthur Andersen had a hidden profit agenda. Some people thought Arthur Andersen wanted to buy the school district. Why else would members of the firm be donating their time and funding some of the events? What was in it for Arthur Andersen to engage with Alameda as a partner? John Searles, the former superintendent, liked to joke that he tried to sell the district but nobody wanted to buy it. Clark indicated that the Arthur Andersen participants walked into the relationship with the clear understanding that they were not a funding agent. Arthur Andersen had its own long-term business interests, investing in developing the talent at the end of the educational pipeline. Members of the firm were quite clear on this long-term business strategy, but they were also acting as civic-minded players in the community. "In that respect," Clark explains, "I think the relationship between Arthur Andersen and AUSD began as a healthier, adult-to-adult rather than . . . parent-to-child relationship. It really came from an attitude that we were equal partners."

Expanding and Managing the Partnership

The Andersen-Alameda partnership—like the Lesher-Norpac alliance—is based on a shared vision and strong interdependence among its stakeholders. Arthur Andersen was interested in gathering more local businesses together to share in its commitment. Expanded involvement from the business community came as a result of a presentation Nancy Clark and her colleagues made about their work with Alameda. About a week later, Arthur Andersen received a call from AT&T's public relations department, requesting a meeting. As a result, AT&T gave $50,000 to help fund a program at Alameda that probably would otherwise have been a victim of budget cuts. The money was dedicated to a project at two schools to design a learning system that is developmentally paced rather than based on students' age. Teachers working on this project were inspired to do what they had been trained to do in college—they now had the tools and resources to work on the real needs of children and the community rather than working from some predetermined curriculum. Some children, for instance, are ready to read by four years of age, while others aren't ready until they're eight. If they have a bad experience at four, because they aren't ready developmentally, they will often feel frustrated with learning, or they will be pigeonholed as slow.

Another example Clark offered of the partners' shared vision concerns the inclusion of total-quality practices in the school system. Arthur Andersen brought in David Langsford, a widely recognized authority on the total-quality method, to work with the Alameda staff. His work has challenged their thinking about how to address the quality of education—which really has to do with the instructional and management philosophies of our school systems. Langsford's insights encourage a philosophy (and practice) of continuous improvement within a total school system.

In other words, schools need to partner with the kids. There's a saying that describes the traditional school as a place "where kids come to watch adults work." Clark observes that "we have to learn to work *with* the kids rather than be at odds with the ways in which they learn as individuals. If they become involved in their own learning or they have to teach someone else, they'll retain eighty to one hundred percent of it. It's the system we have to work on, . . . creating learning systems where we're collaborating more, working in teams, understanding how to improve our own learning . . . to be more self-managing."

An example of involving kids in their own learning and using tools to ensure the quality of that learning occurred with one of the district's second grade teachers, Mary Dierking. She had been working with her kids, outside the curriculum, on ways to improve the quality of the school. Mary reports that she participated in David Langsford's training in the spring of 1993: "I was invited because I am a mentor teacher in the system. I truly believe this would have never happened had it not been for our partnership with Arthur Andersen. Nancy Clark found out about David, and Arthur Andersen contracted with him to work with us. Our training with David focused on giving our children the tools to become self-directed learners. This notion is very much tied to our philosophy that children be responsible for their own learning, . . . learn ways to access the knowledge."

As a result of this training, Mary and her colleagues were encouraged to try new things. According to Mary:

> It's very exciting. This year I worked with my students to assess what they learned last year and engaged them in defining what they want to learn this year . . . to think about why they come to school every day. One kid said, "I want to learn science," and one of the others said, "Well, if we're going to learn science, we have to learn math first." So you see, they get involved in planning the curriculum priorities for the year; they have thought through the building blocks of why they're learning what they learn, and have a better understanding of why. It's all very motivating.

In 1993 Mary decided to apply some of the tools for analyzing and increasing quality that she learned in David Langsford's training session to a major school problem—at least as perceived by the students. As a team, the students made lists of what they liked and didn't like. One of the things they identified that they didn't like was lunchroom behavior. They used a number of quality tools to look at all of the different elements of lunchroom behavior, like yelling and screaming, spilling food, and so on. They decided they wanted to work on litter, defined what they meant by litter, then came up with measurements. Mary describes the evolution of these students' learning:

> Next they worked out an effective approach to dealing with this problem. At the time of each lunch period, the students on the team would count the litter at each table before and after lunch. Once they collected the data, they put it into graphs, providing evidence of a large variation between the before and the after. The second-graders who participated in this team shared the lunchroom with a group of fourth-graders. They came into the lunchroom *after* the older kids. As a result of charting and graphing the litter left behind from both groups, the second-grade group discovered that they left as much litter in the lunchroom as the fourth-graders.
>
> As a result of their self-discovery, they decided to correct their own behavior. The students came up with several possible solutions. They would sit in assigned seats so they could measure their own progress, they would each be accountable for cleaning up their own mess, and then someone would be assigned to be the last one out, ensuring that the entire room was clean. Then they went to the fourth-graders and engaged them in cleaning up their mess. The rules in the lunchroom were that, once [the students were] finished with lunch, the principal would excuse them to the playground. As a further extension of being responsible for cleaning up after themselves, the students later cut a deal with the principal to determine for themselves when they broke away for recess. They didn't have to wait to be excused.

The students made all of these changes and then graphed the results. They found a large decrease in litter left in the lunchroom. In addition, yelling, kicking, and other annoying behavior declined as well. More amazing, though, was that the kids who took the leadership role on this project would, historically, never have stood up in front of a group. One of the three who made a presentation was a stutterer, one had had a stroke when he was five and had trouble with linear thought, and the child who did the data gathering had spent most of his first year in the principal's office for bad behavior. These are the kind of kids teachers have tried desperately to connect with. Clark asserts that "our future success as a country will be measured by how well the majority eighty percent of our students achieve, as well as the top ten to twenty percent."

Although monitoring lunchroom litter is not part of the academic curriculum, monitoring behavior is an important part of learning: learning how they do things, discovering how they really behave, correcting it, negotiating new rules, engaging their peers in new behavior, working as a team—such learning processes are often as important as what students specifically learn in terms of content. According to Mary Dierking, without Arthur Andersen's help the teachers and staff in Alameda would never have explored these alternative approaches to student learning. This kind of problem solving is much more common in business than in education. The Alameda teachers and staff could have fought against the alien, business-oriented approaches to learning that were offered by Arthur Andersen. Instead they all learned different, respected perspectives and opinions in the process of coming together to work on a common problem.

Hearing that Arthur Andersen used the same approach to improve its hiring practices validated the broad-based application of this method for the Alameda teachers. Dierking noted that stories about business's use of these learning principles forced her to realize that business is looking for men and women with broad-based skills, for people who seek challenges, take risks, adapt to change, and know how to solve problems, in addition to having the more traditional academic knowledge. "It made me focus," said Mary, "on how important these other skills are for the child's education, even at the second-grade level."

This experience gave Mary Dierking and her colleagues a new

perspective and expanded their thinking about teaching and learning. The kids came away with a stronger feeling of competence about their ability to self-teach. They were more engaged not only in what they learned, but in why and how they learned it. They could see the value in change. They became partners in their own education. Dierking thinks that she and her colleagues now need to learn to share more information with each other. Teachers can become partners with each other, creating support groups and using each other as resources in trying new things. The challenge lies in that teachers already feel put-upon, as Dierking illustrates:

> Nancy Clark and I tried to pull together a group of teachers who had been through the Langsford training earlier this year. We didn't have a very good showing. It was after school, in May, close to the end of the school year. So in our current mind-set, we were adding more to what already feels like an overloaded schedule. In some ways it's our mind-set that has to change more than our schedule. We have to reset our priorities—letting go of stuff that no longer adds value to the kids and the teachers and engaging in things that will make a difference.

Benefits of the Partnership

Nancy Clark notes that the partnership, as with any relationship, is experiencing different phases of change and transition as it evolves. From the spring through early fall of 1993 the partnership experienced a lull:

> I was working on other projects and the new superintendent, Dennis Chaconas, was transitioning into the district. We did not know each other, and we didn't have much time together. It was not until Dennis and I got together that we began to reignite our partnership. This was critical if we were going to continue to work together. I was concerned about Arthur Andersen's ongoing role, as well as our need

to bring on additional business partners. With more partners [involved], a shared vision and philosophy and clearly defined roles and responsibilities are paramount to a healthy working relationship and successful results. As we expand, there is more comfort and support that the change agent role is shared by all of us who are involved, and not just dependent on Arthur Andersen.

The hope is that we continue to strengthen the partnership, so that each member can ebb and flow with the needs of the district and the demands of the various constituents without impeding our collective results. Each of us needs to be committed to the bigger picture, to a win-win for the whole; otherwise we will all fail. Too often, schools and districts have been promised support by the broader community, only to find themselves alone again within a few months. I want to make sure that we as business partners do not disappoint the district by raising expectations and then failing to deliver. To do that, we must be realistic with each other and work together in ways that provides value for each of us and for the whole system.

Even the selection process for the new superintendent underscored how different this project has been. Fifty people have participated in developing the criteria, and hundreds have been canvassed. The new superintendent has been hired on condition that he continue to make this partnership happen. What the partners have created together has served as an excellent foundation for the next stage of leadership in Alameda. Four of the five board members have come to Nancy Clark to express their deep appreciation for the work that Arthur Andersen has done.

Dennis Chaconas, Alameda's new superintendent of schools, certainly seems to exemplify the continuity of this remarkable alliance. He readily indicated his full support for the partnership: "I'm possessed. I joined Alameda because of the work that came out of our joint visioning project. The student profile is where we need to be." Chaconas believes that education is close to where the car industry was ten years ago: "We have a credibility gap. In our case, and in reference to our partnership with Arthur Andersen, we all realize and feel a bit frustrated that there hasn't been as much implementation against the vision as everyone had hoped for."

Alameda's challenge now, according to Chaconas, is to move the vision into the school sites and classrooms. To do that, the system must engage more people and be more aggressive in driving the agenda: "The way I see it, together with the board, we have to set some broad goals, we have to evaluate ourselves against our goals and have explicit time lines."

Nancy Clark suggests that the partners are still in a learning mode, although they are beginning to see real change at the classroom level. For example, in 1993 the school system went through some horrendous budget cuts. The system convened a cross-section of the community to look at the criteria to be used in making these cuts. Although the cuts were painful, the partners were able to use their earlier work in the school system as a backdrop for the decisions that were made regarding where to cut. People in the system worked together to determine the cuts to be made.

Arthur Andersen and the Alameda Unified School District have made sure they can count on each other. Each partner has delivered what it said it would. The partnership continues to show progress, and the new superintendent would like to secure continued resources from Arthur Andersen to move the project along. Chaconas, however, also identified many challenges that his school system and the partnership now face. First, change is uncomfortable. Being in a rut is predictable. It is a mind-set, but one that often hinders the drive to change. In addition, the school system overspent by $8 million in 1993. The system had to borrow funds from the state, and it has until 1996 to pay back these funds. Chaconas indicates that he "will have to walk a tightrope between recognizing our progress and being unrelenting about what's still to be done. That will unravel some people."

Chaconas also indicates that he needs to become the champion for this partnership effort. He must keep the partners focused on the graduate profile so the school system can evaluate its progress as the partnership continues to work on various issues. He must "be the Pied Piper with my constituents and be 'hands on' in my efforts to reinforce the vision at the grass roots, where it has to take hold. As we move closer to the sites and into the classrooms, it's important that we always ask ourselves about the impact of what we're doing on the kids. . . . In the end, do our kids feel better?" Chaconas offers as an example the decision to lengthen the school day, which resulted in more discipline problems and teacher burnout. In the end, according to Chaconas, the Alameda school system must be a customer-driven business. "We can learn [about customer orientation] from companies like Arthur Andersen."

When asked what steps should be taken to move the Arthur Andersen–Alameda Unified School District partnership to its next phase, Michael Doyle first identified change as the major force driving this project. The Alameda school system was being forced to rethink itself. Members of the Alameda community were coming to the realization that quality education is at the core of their community's health and well-being. We can't envision long-term success for our businesses without rethinking the future of our schools. The Alameda schools were struggling for adequate funding—as were most public schools. John Searles, the superintendent, had at the time just had his contract renewed by the board by a slim margin. The depressed California economy was causing scarce funds to shrivel even more. The Navy, a major employer in Alameda, was being forced to close its bases. It was a perfect setting for innovation. What's now needed, according to Doyle, is for the two leaders of this initiative to together become champions for extending the project into a new phase:

> I think if we don't have that it will hobble along and die. Dennis Chaconas, the newly hired superintendent, and Dick Measelle, Arthur Andersen's managing director, need to take the lead, to develop a strategy that is mutually beneficial. Arthur Andersen will

need to recommit some resources at the partner level. Nancy Clark is raising funding from other locally based businesses. Alameda Schools needs to show some results from this last phase and demonstrate a continuous commitment to making the vision happen. They need to demonstrate that their vision is getting implemented. For example, to what extent is the quality model being used in both the administration and in the classroom? How are the school principals being held accountable for the vision? To what extent are ungraded classes, chartered schools, technological changes, developmental learning practices happening?

In terms of the evolution of organizations, Doyle suggests that the Alameda schools are at the dying stage—as are most public schools. Alameda is trying to start a new life cycle. According to Doyle, it has some momentum: "Of the thirteen to fifteen percent of the stakeholder population that we need to drive the change effort so it really begins to affect the system, we probably have engaged four to five percent. That means we have to continue the effort before we lose too much ground or momentum."

When asked what he thinks will be the future role for Arthur Andersen in this partnership, Tom Kelly, western region managing director for Arthur Andersen, indicates that in the near future the firm must refocus its commitment. Kelly firmly believes that the leaders of the Alameda school system must drive the change:

In the long run they have to be empowered with enough resource and money and ability to do things without Sacramento bureaucrats' getting in their way. That has to get fixed. There is the potential to fix it. I wouldn't bet on it, but it is possible. In the meantime there has been considerable sharing of information and knowledge. There is a lot of sharing that has gone on in building the vision and goals, and we are now in the action stage. There is not enough deep action yet. It is still a bit too anecdotal. We see some changed behaviors in the classroom. We see some students that appear to be reacting in a positive way in the short term. Their behaviors seem to improve. But until you see the profile, until you see what comes out of the pipeline twelve years later, you'll never know. And we don't have metrics for measuring success in the short term. It is a long-term commitment.

Kelly thinks the project and the Alameda school system are on the right path. As with any other change, Kelly believes that this effort is always in need of a catalyst: "I don't think [Arthur Andersen] can be the driver. At one point we were the driver. I think we can be a catalyst. I don't think we can continue to be the driving force."

Kelly expressed his concern about the recent closing of the Alameda military bases. It was an important part of the economy. The sheer economics of what is going to hit these communities over the next two or three years could collapse this project and the financial structure of the school system. Teachers won't be hired, or existing teachers will be laid off; some of the schools participating in this project may be closed down. Kelly doesn't think that Arthur Andersen can solve a problem of that magnitude.

Kelly recommends that two or three new partners be found for this project. These individuals (leaders of major organizations) should be younger, with children. They should also be East Bay residents who will have a sense of ownership and will work closely with Alameda's leaders. "If we have people involved who have a personal stake in sustaining the health of the community system that supports these schools," Kelly says, "they might help them carry it through."

According to Kelly, Dennis Chaconas, as Alameda's superintendent, is very strong: "The initial vision only lasts so long. It needs to be revitalized and refreshed. . . . I think there is a good shared vision. I don't think the structural issues have been dealt with. I think there are some driving forces, partially weakened. Right now we are working to help the superintendent and the

Alameda community reach a new level in the reinvention process."

Kelly thinks Chaconas is a visionary leader, and that, along with several dedicated teachers, Chaconas should be able to revitalize the project. Certainly a partnership of such timely importance, given the problems facing American schools, is worthy of such dedication and vision.

Chapter Eight

The Council for Continuous Improvement

A Multi-Industry, Multisector Consortium

According to Pat Reilly, the founder of the Council for Continuous Improvement (CCI), his role with the council got started with companies that were clients of his consulting business. As an external consultant, he would often work with companies in the same industry; he gained enough perspective to see the similarities in the problems they faced, and therefore the kind of opportunities to be garnered from working together. According to Reilly, "We could put a tape recorder down in the middle of a table, change the name of the company, turn on the tape recorder—and their concerns, problems, and opportunities would all sound pretty much the same. Eighty to ninety percent of the time they were struggling with the same issues, but they all thought their issues were different. 'What we do here has little to do with what you do over there.' It was a real separatist mentality."

Given their similarities, Reilly saw the potential for these companies to be a rich resource for one another, if they would share information and form a kind of "expert system" they could all tap into. That was the basic concept behind CCI. During that time the semiconductor industry was struggling with the complexities of global competition. As a result, industry leaders were receptive to meeting with their peers, and their competition, to share experiences and document their discussions.

Getting Started: Formation of the Partnership

Reilly speaks about his "humble beginnings," but CCI began, in 1989, with several major companies: Intel, Texas Instruments, Motorola,

National Semiconductor, VLSI, Varian, Northern Telecom, and Pat's own consulting firm, Jones, Reilly and Associates. Participants in the early meetings were often concerned about sharing what is commonly viewed as proprietary information. But they balanced this concern with a recognition of the value of sharing ideas and insights into different manufacturing and business processes. Reilly suggests that the participants found the initial sessions to be beneficial because the dialogue enabled them to "collectively understand how to improve [their] business in ways that [helped them] become stronger competitive forces, not only as separate companies but as a unified force within the semiconductor industry."

In this initial, discovery phase, there was a strong focus on learning from each other. The participating companies began to realize that in the past they were often buying their wisdom and insights (and in many instances their common assumptions) from consultants. Through their collaborative efforts they began to leverage their collective wisdom. Reilly noted that "this was a significant shift in mind-set! Companies that had historically considered themselves arch rivals were coming together to share information that they once considered proprietary."

A second issue behind the founding of this partnership was that people in these companies felt they were being "jerked around" by their customers, which were the companies they supplied. As vendors, semiconductor companies are often forced to comply with redundant and conflicting standards. The participants in CCI knew that some uniform way of responding would make their lives a lot easier. They had to figure out an appropriate way of approaching common problems imposed from the outside. They believed that each organization should have internal measures strong enough to ensure that the customer receives consistent product quality. The leaders of these semiconductor companies believed that collectively, through learning and sharing, they could take charge of their own internal processes in a more effective manner.

A third benefit they anticipated from this venture was the formal documentation of what they were learning and creating together. Prior to the formation of CCI, there were no databases or libraries that semiconductor companies could go to for guidelines and instructions on running certain operations. "I mean, you got snippets everywhere," Reilly says. "You've got something in a book, something in a journal, something in a speech, something in a conference, something in a phone call. We got little pieces of information scattered all over that would be nice if [they] were collected and accessible." Documenting their collective wisdom on some of their common processes would be of benefit to them all.

Several themes were emphasized in the initial partnership: the desire to learn from each other, the need to develop a consistent approach to assure quality, and the desire to document common knowledge (build an "expert system"). These themes stimulated the building of core competencies for the council. In starting CCI the participants, according to Reilly, "literally closed the doors for the first year. We didn't accept any new members. We said, 'Let's just see if we can do this. If we can do this, then we'll announce it. If we can't do this, no one will be the wiser.' So we really began as an experiment to discover what worked, and this initial partnership of companies became the foundation for what the CCI member companies have created for themselves."

Structuring the Partnership

In August 1991 Pete Hamm was "loaned" to CCI by one of its member companies, IBM, to lead the council through the next stage in its evolution. Early in 1992 CCI experienced some structural changes, typical of an organization experiencing exponential growth and making the resulting changes required in its business practices. During CCI's early formation, Pat Reilly held formal leadership roles both in his own consulting firm and at CCI. The symbiotic nature of these two organizations was integral to CCI's growth. Clearly the early alliance between the original member companies might never have catalyzed and gained momentum without Reilly's time, nurturing, and knowledge base in the fields of statistical process control, quality assurance, and continuous improvement.

By the first quarter of 1992 CCI's membership continued to grow, and the partnership had broader public exposure. Membership on the CCI board of directors (elected by CCI's member companies) rotated, and the profile of CCI's leadership took on a broader, more formal business perspective. The board began to question the closely held working and financial affiliation between Jones, Reilly and Associates, a for-profit consulting firm, and CCI, a nonprofit organization. Reilly's dual role became problematic. Faced with the perceived conflict of interest in his two roles, Reilly left CCI's board, physically relocated, and moved into a role as a vendor to the organization.

Two years later, in August 1993, Pete Hamm was formally named as president and chief executive officer of CCI. In his formalized role he is responsible for the direction and operations of this rapidly expanding national cooperative. CCI's formal mission now is "to develop, document, and share improvement methodologies and implementation systems that its members can use to continually improve their products, services, and operational performance." The board's vision for this national partnership of public and private enterprise is "to be the preeminent member-driven national consortium for the continuous improvement of all aspects of management processes and operational performance."

In August 1991 CCI had 29 member companies. By 1994 it boasted over 168 members, representing between one and two million American workers. Membership grows at a rate of four or five new members every month. According to Hamm, "By 1995 we could easily have two hundred member companies."

The council has as a small staff of seven people and a nine-member board of directors that is representative of its member companies. In keeping with the concept of a flat, highly networked organization, a lot of its core activities—identification and research of problems and opportunities common to its member companies, training and facilitation, and documentation—are outsourced to its member companies or to subcontractors. CCI has targeted five geographic regions it would like to serve. In addition to the central office, in Santa Clara, California, there is now a regional office in southern California and in Texas, with future plans to open three others for the purpose of better serving CCI's constituents.

Since its inception in 1989, CCI's membership has grown increasingly diverse. CCI currently serves manufacturing companies, service companies, academia, and government. The primary reason for membership is an interest in continuous improvement applied to the operational and managerial aspects of an enterprise, coupled with an interest in sharing knowledge and learning from others. According to Hamm, "We expect our members to contribute their experiences and some of their efforts as volunteers in support of the organization and each other. Membership entails three things: an offering of training-related products and services, formal and informal access to a network of companies that share a basic interest in continuous improvement practices and methodologies, and expertise in team management training and group facilitation. The majority of the products are workshops, developed by the members themselves, and are designed to be self-prompting so they can be used inside companies without the need for an external instructor."

One of CCI's main services is to provide public forums for its members to come together to share experiences on continuous improvement and management issues. An outgrowth of this is the development of training products by cross-industry teams composed of member companies organized around special interest groups. Once the teams develop the products, using real-world experience, they are distributed to all CIC member companies. Master copies are distributed under a unique copyright agreement for companies to use internally in any way they choose. Between 1991 and 1994, the number of documented training materials has virtually doubled from twenty-two to forty-three, encompassing a wide variety of key topics such as team facilitation, business process improvement, benchmarking, design of experiments, and advanced statistical process control.

CCI's public forums are conducted once every quarter in different regions across the country, attracting between 250 and 600 people from CCI's membership. During these sessions there is a general forum that provides a forum, called Call to Action, where members can raise a question or problem they have encountered in their work, announce recent work they have completed, or identify a topic they have a special interest in and need information on. During these sessions, participants break into twelve to sixteen special interest groups (SIGs) to share and codevelop information, workshops, and training materials for their own use on topics of mutual interest. This public forum provides a regular opportunity for individuals and companies to work in partnership to address common concerns.

Reilly and Hamm have witnessed a significant transformation in CCI during its first five years, as it established itself as a viable national organization. According to Hamm, the transition was rocky for a while. Faced with the opportunity to rethink Reilly's role within CCI, Pat and Pete have constructed a role for Reilly in which he really excels. He has contracted to work with the council as their lead marketing vendor. His direction is to find new sources of membership.

The circumstances in which CCI finds itself are different today from what they were a few years ago when the partnership was formed. The people are different. The organization is different. The leadership has changed as the requisite skills have changed. The capacity to shift rapidly can often make the difference between success and failure for a partnership. Structurally, CCI is creating models that are very different from those found between most companies today. Paradoxically, and contrary to the conventional mind-set, sharing information across new boundaries makes people and companies better competitors. With globalization the scope of competition is much broader. CCI members are leveraging each other's strengths and expanding their collective vision across public and private sectors.

Driven by leadership initiatives from its members, CCI is willing to explore most any avenue in order to expand its collaborative potential. It engages in endless variations of partnering in order to expand its membership, because as the association expands, its members expand their knowledge base. The association even pursues partnership with other associations. Ironically, these other associations potentially compete for some of the same member companies. Like their member companies, each association has something that it does well. By creating a cross-association alliance, CCI allows expanded access to the information and expertise contained within its membership body.

One example is in the alliance CCI is forming with the American Electronics Association (AEA). In 1992, AEA had about three hundred member companies, two-thirds of them small companies with less than three hundred employees. CCI is a member of AEA, giving its staff access to benefits that are typically available only to large businesses, like group-rate insurance, rental programs, and so on. In turn, AEA is a member organization of CCI, and as a result, AEA's staff members can participate in CCI's networking events and special interest groups (SIGs).

A short time ago, the leaders of AEA realized they had to become more involved with helping their small member companies run their businesses if they were both going to continue to be viable and to survive as an association. Over the years the U.S. electronics market has been eroding as a result of stiffer, worldwide competition. For example, in 1988, 58 percent of the world's electronics products were manufactured in the United States, but by 1992 that percentage had fallen to only 38 percent. At the end of 1992, one in five electronics companies lost money. Profits were down for the third year in a row. Half a million manufacturing jobs had been lost in the preceding five years, and over the same period, the U.S. share of the world electronics market had fallen some three percent each year. Projecting these trends out to the year 2006, there is not much future for companies the size of the majority of AEA's members.

Small, emerging electronics companies don't have the capital, the competence, nor the leverage of their larger competitors to sustain a competitive advantage. Hence they must partner with their own competitors to rethink their future—in order to compete, ironically. As one member put it, AEA knew that the bread of survival was buttered on both sides. Towards that end, Craig Walter, AEA's new senior vice president of quality resources (on loan to AEA from Hewlett-Packard), talked to more than one hundred of its member companies to find out what they needed. As a result of what they heard, AEA launched a total-quality-commitment initiative, with emphasis on providing opportunities for its member companies to forge deeper business alliances. The goal is to bring world-class practices from the industry's best and largest companies to AEA's membership in order to increase their competitiveness and increase their shareholder value. "Our charter was to do something that would have significant impact on multiple companies," said AEA's Walter. At the time that the AEA was defining the need for quality and continuous improvement practices for its member companies, CCI was approaching AEA to look at how they might make their services more available to smaller companies (that is, AEA's members) that couldn't afford to pay single-member fees.

In concert with the explorations between CCI and AEA, several other layers of partnerships were forming within AEA. In 1991, five member companies and a host of consultants began to meet in Portland, Oregon. In 1992, a program called Partnership for Competitiveness (PFC) was launched as a collaborative effort among the five company presidents and consultants to learn and implement affordable strategies and techniques used by the world's best electronics companies. A detailed road map was developed for implementation of the program's initiatives. AEA estimates that during the first year alone over two thousand hours of volunteer time was contributed to the start-up of this new venture.

Sponsored by the Oregon Council for the AEA, supported by the accounting and consulting firm of Arthur Andersen, and administered by John Bernard, a consultant and the executive vice president of World Class Management, Inc., the partnership brings together management teams from independent companies to pursue total-quality management. Participating companies commit to a three-year partnership that includes training, consultation, and financial support for the program.

"The first thing we did," John Bernard explains, "was to write up a set of covenants to the vision we had established together. These two things have been more important to our success than you could possibly imagine. Our relationship will be only as good as the vision for our collaboration and the trust represented in our covenants. Our purpose was to share resources for our mutual long-term gain." As a pilot three-year program, PFC's focus is to move its partner companies from an internal focus to one that is customer-driven. The total-quality-management road map guides the member companies through preparation, development, and integration of quality management. According to the blueprint developed by the founding Oregon partners, members will complete core training, set future visions, and define systems to reach its goals during the first year of operation. In the second year, members will refine the guidelines to meet more in-depth requirements. And in the third year they will develop more formal management processes that link closely with customer satisfaction and marketplace competitiveness.

According to Mike Bosworth, president and chief executive officer of OrCAD, one of PFC's partners, this process is "PHW—plain hard work. Work that requires commitment and a practical vision of what can be accomplished." And rethinking how one does business does require a leap of faith. Other member companies in this venture include Wayne Ross, president and CEO of Micropump; Planar Systems and its CEO, Mac McDonnell; Etec Systems and its general manager, Paul Warkentin; and Althin Medical and its vice president and general manager, Chuck Albert.

While the five members of the PFC shared a conviction that profound, even radical, improvement was essential to their competitiveness, there was little else, at first blush, that they had in common. True, they were all relatively small technology companies. But it was there that the similarities ended. The differences in what these companies did was less an issue than the similarities in their goals and in what they needed to achieve those goals. As Micropump's Wayne Ross puts it, "Our companies are different, but we need to learn similar things."

Each of the five companies were attracted to PFC for different reasons. Bosworth's OrCAD, for example, had been through some turbulent times. What had begun as an entrepreneurial software company now faced the challenge of moving to the "next level." To grow, the company needed to transform itself with a more disciplined approach to product development and delivery and a keener focus on the customer and the competition. Furthermore, the company's culture had evolved into one of isolated departments and functions, and that was an obstacle to growth. "I felt we needed a broad transformation within OrCAD," says Bosworth.

Bosworth was also attracted to the partnering aspect of PFC. "There's obvious value in working with other companies," he says.

There's support, sharing, and mutual learning. There's also positive peer pressure that brings discipline to the process. On your own, it's easy enough to put things off; when you know that your partners are doing their homework, you're determined to do your own. And of course, there's the economy of scale. We're all relatively small companies with limited resources to spend, for example, in training and total quality. By pooling our resources, we're able to train over five hundred people in over thirty courses. The money we invest in PFC,

some $4,300 per company per month, is less than what I'd spend just
on an adequate training program. With the PFC, I get exceptional
training as well as orientation to total-quality management.

Micropump, explains Wayne Ross, is a company in transition,
moving from mechanical to electronic products. In turn, the move
to new types of products means a move to new markets and new
customers. With little direct competition, the challenge for Micropump is to "compete with itself," by constantly improving its own
internal processes. Ross, too, likes the discipline the PFC provides.
He also feels the PFC is a "safe place" to learn about partnering and
partnering skills—skills that will be mandatory in the marketing
environment of the 1990s and beyond.

For Paul Warkentin and Etec Systems, there was already an
existing commitment to continuous improvement; but PFC offered
critical-mass advantages that Etec, by itself, could not realize. With
the PFC, says Warkentin, "Training isn't done 'to us' but is instead
demand-driven. We actively participate in defining the nature and
timing of the training we need to make Etec successful. With TQM
[total-quality management], people have a much more concrete
understanding of their role within our overall strategic plan. As a
result, people make decisions and communicate with one another
in ways that support our company's competitiveness."

Planar Systems was probably the most sophisticated team member in its existing approach to quality management. But "things
were too ad hoc," says Planar's McDonnell. "I wanted a more formal, more philosophical foundation in our approach and in our
content. We had the basics; but we had no answer for the 'What's
next?' question. We were feeling pain, but we had no well-defined
pathway. TQM [total-quality management] and PFC's road map
provided that."

PFC Executive Director John Bernard finds there are three
broad categories of executives who are attracted to TQM and to the
unique advantages of the partnership: "First, there are leaders new

to a company who want to encourage a corporate culture focused on the customer and on competitive issues. Then, there are existing leaders who are simply not satisfied with the company's performance. Finally, there are leaders who are aware of the need to improve competitiveness but whose companies aren't currently doing anything formal to achieve that."

Early in the program, the senior executives of each member company agreed on this vision of the Partnership for Competitiveness: "Master challenges and drive incremental and breakthrough improvement to achieve world-class competitiveness using the shared strength of our diverse companies. Inspire ourselves and American industry through our example of successful partnering." "It was the word 'inspire' that created some lively conversations among our members," John Bernard recalls. "But in the end, we agreed that it was right—perhaps more for ourselves than for anyone else." OrCAD's Mike Bosworth puts it this way: "There is a pioneering sense within the PFC. We have the opportunity to create value by helping to fix what's broken with American business. That's going to help our company, and it's going to help other companies. And that *is* inspiring."

The AEA will continue to look for opportunities and locations to "port" this concept. Member companies within the AEA are currently forming the next generation of PFCs, based on the Portland model, having identified California's Silicon Valley as the next launch point. At the same time, CCI is continuing to explore the mutual gain in providing its resources to both AEA's member companies as well as the highly focused PFC model. A partnership between these two associations would assist CCI in tailoring its materials to an ever-expanding marketplace, and could save AEA the costly redundancy of developing their training products from scratch.

Another route for expanding CCI's membership base lies in inventing joint ventures between businesses and academic institutions. "The Council for Continuous Improvement has taken education-industry partnering a step further, to improve themselves and the future work force, by developing college-business partnerships that provide immediate benefits to all parties," according to the February 1994 issue of *Quality*. The article, "Industry-Academe Bond Strengthens," continues: "The program allows a company to sponsor a college or university's CCI membership fee in return for in-kind services . . . such as TQM-related projects, student internships, special studies, research, and surveys."

The University of Chicago School of Business was part of one of the first of these partnerships to emerge from CCI's prospecting, gaining the combined sponsorship of two companies, Square D Co. and Tellabs Operations, Inc. The business school works with Tellabs on assessment diagnostics for groups and teams. With Square D it focuses on the impact of its internal quality education programs. Says William W. Kooser, associate dean for marketing and international programs at the University of Chicago's Graduate School of Business, "Our CCI membership provides us with an unsurpassed opportunity to learn more about the state of quality improvement in business today. It offers us a chance to develop important research relationships with corporations and to simply generate ideas for improving our own operations." According to Bill Englehaupt, manager of total-quality education for Square D, "We want to build a bridge between the university's faculty and our own quality education department, as well as help the University of Chicago connect to the quality community at large."

Square D's student Beth Rosenthal speaks of the incredible opportunity afforded her through this alliance: "They're giving me the ticket to go in and see how all this theoretical stuff is applied. The implementation is something you can't get from the academic world. We're each getting pieces that the other doesn't have" (Dusharme, 1994).

Brigham Young University preceded CCI's venture with the University of Chicago, and it may well have provided the idea that encouraged the council to encourage more partnering between educational institutions and sponsoring companies. Membership for eight hundred faculty and staff from the university's math, engineering, and business schools was paid by a CCI supporter and interested alumnus. A company receiving one of BYU's employees would provide a matching grant as part of the agreement.

In addition to educational institutions, growing numbers of government agencies have joined CCI's membership. This provides a stage for public-private partnerships, where industry and government use CCI meetings as a setting in which they can learn from one another. Corporate partners can learn about becoming better users of government and how to deal with regulatory agencies. At the same time, members from the public sector gain more insight into managing their own operations more efficiently, as well as listening to their corporate customers, who are important consumers of government services. In the fall of 1993, Pat Reilly and Bob Turnbull, CCI's chairman, met with Vice President Gore and his staff on the topic of reinventing government. According to Reilly, "We talked about how industry can be used as a role model for many of the activities that they are looking to initiate within government. We also explored the role of technology and government in building standards and regulations for the national data highway."

According to Turnbull, the second-term chairman of CCI's board,

> There is a natural extension here for CCI. In addition to what we're doing with our member companies, we have an opportunity to contribute to our national competitive agenda. What we've learned from providing a forum for our academic, business, and government institutions to collaborate is that we can share information about practices and principles that were once considered proprietary and still remain fiercely competitive. If our collective principles and practices are so basic and common to all, maybe this represents a void in our educational system. If so, education on cycle-time reduction, reengineering, teamwork, alignment, and partnering should be presented as part of our basic education. In this case we would expand our focus on education.

Turnbull continues by talking about how the United States can remain competitive in a global economy:

> Take Japan, for example. Its education is overly focused on feeding their business and industry, while the U.S. puts enormous emphasis on academia for its own sake. While I don't think we should go overboard like Japan, we could certainly do a better job of putting parts of our educational curriculum to work for us. We could actually exemplify those practices. To play on John Kennedy's message, CCI and our member institutions could be asking ourselves, "What can we do for the nation; what can we do to be influential?" How many organizations can boast a collaborative effort by Motorola, AMD, and IBM to develop the best methods for statistical process controls on the shop floor? The outcome is far greater than any one of these companies could develop on its own. We really believe that the broader our membership, the better we are. The more we are open to learning from each other, the more extensive our impact on the collective knowledge of our public and private markets.
>
> CCI's goal is to provide opportunities to address our country's competitive ability in the global marketplace. If we could assist government and academia in improving their efficiency and effectiveness by 1 percent, the implications could be startling. Working together, we can all become stronger, individually and collectively. We're not building another organization. We are building a capability.

Benefits of the Partnership

What is the value of these expanded pursuits, which take us beyond our traditional boundaries? Why this sudden upsurge in concern for the other guy in a country built on a lone ranger mentality? What are the benefits of partnering in a pressed-for-time environment where we're encouraged to "stick to our knitting"? Bob McIvor, a CCI member and director of final manufacturing at Motorola Corporation, summed it up best: "a win-win for all parties." Motorola has formed multiple partnerships up and down its value chain. According to McIvor, "It's mutually beneficial. We take care of each other's well-being. In the end, everyone wins—most of all the end user."

McIvor indicates that, in his own area at Motorola, partnerships have been established with seven different companies, mostly from the supply side of the value chain. "It's a living thing," he says. "The benefits, in our supply side partnerships, are that we decrease time to market, because our suppliers are involved in the design of [the product]. We develop a friend in need that we can rely on and with whom we have developed a vested interest. It takes time, trust, communication, and sharing. In turn, our vendors get to define new products, which are often leading edge, so they get ahead of their market. We also give them the right of first refusal."

McIvor believes that CCI has been a helpful resource in this movement toward sharing information. As in the case of Lesher and Norpac, one partnership tends to breed other partnerships. McIvor speaks of the informal as well formal benefits that accrue from Motorola's participation in CCI:

> I liken membership with CCI to a self-help charity. It's like a club where you don't really have anything to take until you give something. We have certain common principles that we adhere to. We developed some team training from an existing CCI format. We were an amalgam of different users from different companies and industries. I think what we have created is the best in the country. We all tend to get a little incestuous, always doing things from within. In this case we were all different, but what made the real difference was that we designed and developed what we ended up using. So instead of having some training arm of the company develop something for us, we developed it for ourselves. All of us. Together.

"We are a cooperative for sharing ideas and experiences," says CCI's president and CEO, Pete Hamm. "With the advent of the personal computer, we potentially have a tool to expand our universe, for all of us to interact, learn, and stay informed. We have created an environment where we can learn from each other by sharing our successes and, probably more instructively, our failures. In short, we have nothing to lose and everything to gain as individuals, whole industries, and even a nation engaged in continuously improving how we work together and, as a result, in the quality of our products and services in a global market."

Part Four

What Successful Partnership Requires

Chapter Nine

The Partnership Covenant

Can two walk together, except they be agreed?
—*Amos 3:3*

With regard to ham and eggs, the chicken is
involved; the pig is committed.
—*1980s maxim*

In the many corporate slide presentations we've seen describing current or upcoming partnerships, the agreement is almost always represented in the same way. Instead of a graphic of a contract, a signing ceremony, or people swearing their commitment on a stack of Bibles, we see a simpler, more compelling image—two hands tightly clasped. If the company has an ambitious graphic designer, cuff links with the partners' logos are seen behind the clasped hands. Basically, though, it is the handshake that matters most. The handshake represents a level of commitment and mutual trust that transcends a binding agreement—the handshake suggests not just a contract but a covenant, in the biblical sense. This is probably the most important lesson we learned in our study: covenants (not contracts) lie at the heart of successful partnerships. Even short-term partnerships require a commitment and trust that move beyond the typical legal contract. And long-term partnerships that eventually shift (if successful) from partnerships of function to partnerships of commitment are certainly built on covenants rather than contracts.

In contemporary times, a contract is certainly much more popular and perhaps even more acceptable than a covenant. A contract can readily be broken, while a covenant is enduring and difficult to break. A contract is typically focused on ways to meet the independent needs and interests of each party. A covenant, by contrast, concerns the accomplishment of mutual purposes and a shared mission—as well as independent needs and interests. There is always some higher purpose that lies behind and provides definition for a covenant.

Unfortunately, "covenant" could readily become just another buzzword for business gurus to throw around or corporate dilettantes to pick up—it could become the latest fad, its deeper meaning distorted or misused, as happened to "quality" and "empowerment." There is a long tradition behind the commitment a covenant implies. The marriage vow, for instance, is not a *contract* in the eyes of the church (it is a contract only in the eyes of the state). The marriage ceremony is witnessed by friends and relatives because they are all supposed to form a community of support for the couple, thereby ensuring the lifelong duration of the marriage. This same type of commitment is usually desired by people who form partnerships.

The people we interviewed, for example, constantly brought up their desire to work with others they could trust not only to do their part but also to place the needs of the partnership first. But they were aware, too, that they live in a real world filled with real people. Thus they often told us, they are satisfied with a solid, binding contract. They indicated that a contract is helpful, if not essential, to getting an alliance off on the right track. First, a contract's legally binding nature gives all involved a level of assurance they wouldn't otherwise have. Second, a contract serves as a way to clarify roles, responsibilities, and consequences so that possible future conflicts can be avoided. Formalizing the arrangement, whether by a handshake or a signing ceremony, is normally the last step prospective partners take before entering into a professional alliance. First they flirted with the idea of partnering. Then they chose from among possible mates. Now the focus turns toward the actual commitment. "From this point on," notes one partner in a public relations cooperative, "it's real. That means it's going to hurt sometimes. But, since you're committed, you're bound to shoulder some of that hurt."

But what about the covenant? A partnership moves beyond contract to covenant when an agreement is reached that doesn't just ensure a commitment for a particular period of time and clarify roles and responsibilities, but also provides for three other conditions:

- Information sharing: an ongoing commitment to lowering the boundary between the partnering organizations so information relevant to the partnership is shared freely and in an undistorted manner among the partners.

- Goal clarification: an ongoing commitment to reviewing and reflecting on the operations of the partnership to ensure that it is moving toward appropriate goals and fulfilling the partners' mutual aspirations, and to ensure that emerging goals are given appropriate attention and are built into the partnership's formal planning processes.

- Problem solving: an ongoing commitment to identifying, analyzing, and attempting to solve problems in a collaborative, open manner.

What about our three case-study partnerships: Lesher-Norpac, AUSD–Arthur Andersen, and CCI? To what extent did these partnerships develop covenants rather than contracts? First, in all three partnerships there was a clear commitment to the sharing of appropriate information. The CCI partnership was clearly based from the very first on information sharing, and it soon became a central feature of the Lesher-Norpac partnership. In the case of Andersen-Alameda, the consulting group obviously shared its expertise about how organizations run in an effective and efficient manner, and it applied these principles to its analysis of the school. The Alameda school system leaders also openly shared information about their schools. Any successful consultative partnership requires an open exchange of information, just as any joint venture or consortium, such as Lesher-Norpac or CCI, requires the lowering of boundaries between institutions.

Second, there was also a strong, sustained commitment by all parties in our three case studies to the ongoing clarification (and expansion) of their mutual goals. The Lesher-Norpac partnership appropriately began with a limited set of shared goals. However, as the partnership began to demonstrate real benefits and as its acceptance grew in each organization, the goals of the partnership became more ambitious. In a covenant the original commitment is frequently rearticulated. And a covenant continues to be effective when the commitment is adjusted to accommodate new directions, new learning, and new challenges.

In the case of the Arthur Andersen-Alameda partnership, the goals have remained rather stable; nevertheless, the partners often refer back to these goals to be sure that they are respected by both parties. Ironically, as is the case in many consultative partnerships, one of the goals of the Andersen-Alameda partnership is a reduction in client dependency. Therefore, in this case the covenant will be successfully honored if both parties move toward a dissolution of the relationship, at least in its current form. The covenant is not broken because the client ceases to use the consultant; rather, the termination of the consulting contract is evidence of both partners' ongoing commitment to the covenant and to the continuing growth and maturation of the client.

What about CCI? This consortium is now going through a transition. Its founder, Pat Reilly, has shifted roles, and the consortium is reexamining its goals and aspirations under new leadership. As part of the commitment to continuity and longevity, a covenant often requires a willingness to undergo change and transformation. Partnerships, such as CCI, can rarely remain static—and rarely should, given the particular advantages partnerships offer as flexible, pragmatic associations. It is particularly important that a partnership's goals and purpose are frequently reviewed when it undergoes shifts and adaptations; otherwise, flexibility and pragmatism become nothing more than unanchored, directionless expedience and opportunism.

Finally, we can look to all three partnerships for examples of a commitment to joint problem solving. Such a commitment certainly exists in the Lesher-Norpac partnership—our case study is filled with many examples of collaborative problem solving. Similarly, joint problem solving is at the very heart of the Arthur Andersen-Alameda partnership. Unlike many traditional consultative relationships, the Andersen-Alameda partnership is built not on one-way communication—with expertise and advice flowing from the "knowledgeable" consultant to the "ignorant" client—but rather on the type of mutual, two-way communication that Senge (1990) identifies as "dialogue" (rather than "discussion") among equals. And the CCI partnership, like Andersen-Alameda, seems to hold collaborative problem solving as a central value. Consortia such as CCI exist not so much to share resources as to share expertise and experiences regarding the nature of shared problems and their potential solution.

All three of our case-study partnerships incorporate each of the three central ingredients of a successful covenant. When all three ingredients are in place, mutual trust in the partners' intentions, competence, and perspective are reinforced and enhanced, providing a foundation for a successful partnership. Trust in intentions is enhanced when information is shared; trust in competence is enhanced when problems are mutually addressed and solved; and trust in perspectives is enhanced when goals are monitored, clarified, and expanded with the growth and maturation of a partnership.

Establishing the Covenant

Time and time again in our investigations, we were struck by the sense of solemnity partners felt at the moment they formally made their commitment—when they established their covenant (by whatever name they called it). A number of our interviewees compared the experience to a wedding ceremony, occasionally emphasizing the words "rites," "vows," and "bonds." As one partner in a real estate management firm told us, "If you have any integrity at all, it's a moment you don't take lightly."

One of our original intentions in pursuing this study was to find out how best to formalize a partnership agreement. Does a handshake bind people in ways a legal contract cannot? Is a contract really a better business practice? Are there other ways partners can better demonstrate the depth and breadth of their mutual commitment? We found that there is no one best way for everyone. Just as partnerships vary, so too do the ways partners commit to alliances that are ultimately successful. The nature and form of the initial agreement are entirely up to the people involved.

However, we do suggest that the following six factors be considered when determining the nature of a partnership agreement:

- Size: the bigger the partnership and the organizations that constitute it, the more appropriate it is to complete a formal written agreement that is reviewed and approved by a lawyer.

- Complexity: the more complex the partnership and the organizations that constitute it, the more appropriate it is to complete a detailed, formal agreement.

- Organizational culture: the more formal and bureaucratic the cultures of the organizations that constitute the partnership and the more formal the sector in which the partnership will operate, the more appropriate it is to complete a formal agreement. (For instance, formal agreements are more common between corporations than they are between human service agencies or volunteer groups.)

- Level of turbulence: the more turbulent the environment the partnership will operate in, the more appropriate it is to complete a detailed, formal agreement. (Turbulence is defined as an unpredictable environment in which rapid, undirected change exists alongside stagnation and patterned change.)

- Maturity of the partnership relationship: the less experience the partners have in partnering and the less experience they have in working with one another, the more appropriate it is to complete a detailed, formal agreement that is reviewed and approved by a lawyer.

- Nature of the product or service: the greater the extent to which the product or service offered through the partnership or on behalf of the partnership is uniform and provided in volume, the more appropriate it is to complete a formal, legally binding agreement. (Products and services that frequently change or are custom-designed—for example, artistic collaborations or one-of-a-kind pieces of equipment—often require more flexible, less formal agreements between parties.)

How well were these six factors considered in our three case-study partnerships? First, in all three cases there are formal agreements—though the Lesher-Norpac agreement is much more detailed than that of either Arthur Andersen-Alameda or the CCI partners. Clearly, in the case of Lesher and Norpac, we are talking about two relatively large and complex organizations entering into a rather large (and growing) and complex partnership. Therefore, a carefully detailed agreement was essential. Cultural norms of the Lesher and Norpac corporations also called for a formal agreement, and there was certainly enough uniformity of product (newsprint) and sufficient turbulence in the paper production and newspaper businesses to justify a carefully articulated agreement. We witnessed a gradual diminution in the formality of the relationship, however, as the two partners became increasingly familiar with each other's operations and their mutual trust began to grow. Lesher and Norpac leaders and other participants in the partnership now often make informal agreements regarding site visits and the exchange of information and expertise (not only about those aspects of their operations that are directly related to the partnership, but also about other, less directly related matters, such as increasing worker involvement in the decision-making processes of both companies).

The Arthur Andersen-Alameda partnership brought together one relatively large organization (Alameda) and one relatively small one (Arthur Andersen). Both organizations are rather complex, and their consulting relationship is certainly complex. Most important, however, was the factor of turbulence. The Alameda school system was going through many changes, and its future was definitely unpredictable at the time its partnership with Arthur Anderson was established. A clear, formal agreement was clearly necessary for both parties. Ironically, the traditional cultural norm in many school systems is one of informal collegiality, and the type of service (education) offered by this partnership is variable and individualized. Nevertheless, when school systems such as Alameda come under fire and are threatened from many different sides (teacher unions, public anger, and so on), this collegiality tends to decline, services become more uniform, and formality becomes much more important.

In the case of Anderson and Alameda, it was also important that the agreement remain formal, even once the two partners had gotten to know each other better and had built a firm foundation of trust. Consultants should always maintain a formal relationship with their clients; otherwise, it is very easy for them to fall into the organizational traps that exist within the organization. Like the therapist who falls in love with his or her patient, the consultant who develops an informal relationship, without reflection, with a client is not providing very good service. Friendships are perfectly acceptable; but some critical distance must always exist between the client and the consultant in a consultative partnership.

CCI, on the other hand, exhibited a minimal need for a complex, detailed agreement; however, there did have to be a formal agreement of some sort, for the consortium could not exist or effectively plan or administer itself without a formal, legal commitment to the paying of dues, consulting fees, conference fees, and so forth. As we expected, there were many informal agreements among members of the consortium in their individual interactions—an expedient vehicle for sharing information and expertise is, after all, one of the great appeals of any consortium or user group. Therefore, although the relationship between the consortium and its participating members must be formal, care must be taken not to let this formality get in the way of the critical informality of the consortium participants' variable, independent interactions.

Though many of these six factors apply in the formation of most partnership agreements, at the very heart of any partnership agreement are the issues of flexibility and pragmatism: Are the "ties that bind" too binding? Are the contractual agreements drawn up by the partners too confining for them? Are the partners able to adjust to changes in the internal or external environment of their business? Conversely, are these ties a sign of commitment and continuity? Do they allow the partnership to be highly flexible without becoming fragmented, and pragmatic without becoming too expedient and directionless? In beginning to examine in some detail the nature of partnership agreements, therefore, we must first look at the issues of flexibility and pragmatism. We can then turn to the various ways partners formulate their agreements—both formal and informal.

Flexibility and Pragmatism

The men and women we interviewed consistently told us that flexibility is essential to successful partnerships. As we noted in Chapter One, flexibility is one of the major reasons for entering a partnership; it provides a distinct advantage in a highly competitive marketplace. Flexibility is possible in a partnership when that key ingredient—trust—is present. Trust (in one's partners' intentions, competency, and perspective) permits greater responsiveness to changing or uncertain conditions. Successful partners can readily reconfigure their relationship and their mutual business because they trust one another and because they have established a covenant based on the sharing of information, continuing clarification of goals, and mutual problem solving. Each of these three components of a covenant are particularly salient when partners are shifting directions and being pragmatically flexible.

Such flexibility is apparent in the Lesher-Norpac partnership. The two companies established an initial set of contracts regarding the sole-source supply of newsprint, but they have since adjusted their relationship to expand their areas of cooperation and the scope of their partnership. In a partnership, where there is shared problem solving and shared responsibility, everyone pitches in to get the job done and to meet the needs of the moment. Even though the partners may have specific areas of specialization or interest, they all have one common goal—namely, keeping the strategic relationship afloat and prospering. Thus the partners' pragmatism is the very thing that allows them to maintain the flexibility that will help the partnership succeed.

In the case of the Council for Continuous Improvement, this meant setting aside rivalries, different perspectives on the business, and traditional barriers in order to provide access to a common base of information about industry performance: pragmatism demanded flexibility. This relationship between flexibility and a pragmatic goal is similar to what architects speak of as "form following function." A focus on function is particularly valuable when a business is working at either extreme—when it is going through hard times or when it is thriving and scrambling to keep up with demand. A pragmatic attitude in a partnership is revealed not only in the partners' flexible responses to changing conditions and their willingness to let form follow function, but also in a strong work ethic within the partnership. Successful partners are committed to and typically become personally accountable for the partnership they helped to form. Furthermore, they have each other around to ensure that this commitment and investment of energy does not waiver. This work ethic is often manifested by the "no borrowing, no debt" attitude of many partners. While they may borrow heavily for their own individual company, they often don't want to be beholden to anyone—like bankers and loan officers—with regard to their partnership. This may be a primary reason many organizations seek out a partnership in the first place: benefits are acquired with minimal ongoing financial commitments. We certainly found this "pay as you go" mentality at work in the Lesher-Norpac partnership. Each partner made sure that there were some immediate tangible financial benefits associated with participation in the partnership. Similarly, the partners in CCI looked for early tangible benefits. Only in the case of the Arthur Anderson-Alameda school system partnership did we find a willingness to defer benefits for either partner for a long period of time.

Turning to our interviewers, we find that the owners of BiChip, the small high-tech company in partnership with the much larger firm TechnoCorp, have placed a consistently strong emphasis on moderation in formulating and executing their business decisions. One of the company's officers made it clear BiChip's policy right from the outset was fiscal conservatism: "pay as we go." Since the company's founders elected to avoid support from profit-driven venture capitalists in favor of a more freedom-driven path, they had to move carefully and deliberately. They were paid by TechnoCorp as they met specific milestones in the creation of their first product for the partnership; this provided them with a modest income while keeping them totally focused on delivering the product.

Sealed with a Handshake

Some of the people we interviewed never felt the need to commit to a legally binding agreement in their partnership. For them, a personal agreement—usually signified by a handshake—was enough. As might be expected, these kinds of arrangements tended to predominate in partnerships of commitment. Marilyn and Kathleen, the two women who established a partnership between their management and career-development consulting firms, are able to remain flexible in part because they are friends. "I never worry about fees or contracts," says Marilyn. "I've never signed one with Kathleen." Kathleen added that, while she usually feels the need to sign a contract with the clients both women serve, she too has never felt the need to do so with Marilyn's firm. In this case the high level of trust shared by the partners is the result of a long and close preexisting relationship. Neither Marilyn or Kathleen are, in principle, against the idea of contracts. In fact, both of their firms rely on formal, legally binding contracts in their dealings with vendors and clients. However, because they have known each other for a long time and because they trust each other implicitly, neither Marilyn or Kathleen see a contract as necessary to the success of their partnership.

While it can be an immensely positive experience to forge a partnership based on this level of trust, we found that it's critical to be honest about the nature of the relationship at the partnership's base. In several cases, for example, we learned that people had committed to contract-free partnerships with family members or friends more out of timidity than trust. In founding a financial service partnership with a company owned by his best friend, one of our informants told us that he was "a little nervous about not spelling things out right up front. But we'd been friends so long, I felt I'd be insulting him. My guess is that he probably felt the same about me."

While partnerships formed without formal contracts are more prevalent among small family- and friendship-based businesses, they can also be found among large organizations. Kingston Technology Corporation, the computer upgrader cited in Chapter Two, is an excellent example. While the company did half a billion dollars' worth of business in more than thirty countries during 1993— nearly twice as much as in 1992—and relies on a network of dozens of strategic partners, its president, John Tu, claims to do almost all company business on a handshake.

According to Tu, the reason lies in a deep-seated dislike for lawyers and the large fees they charge, both for drawing up contracts and then for settling contract disputes. In fact, he takes great pride in forming a big round zero with his thumb and forefinger when he's asked how many lawyers he's hired (Meyer, 1993). Complementing Tu's desire to save money on legal fees is, we believe, an equally strong desire to earn the trust of his company's strategic partners, by openly sharing capital, know-how, and markets—much as is the case with Lesher and Norpac. The thinking seems to be that—even in the big leagues—the best way to get absolute trust is to give absolute trust. Kingston Technology and the Lesher-Norpac partnership prove that this strategy can be extremely successful, regardless of a company's size.

Of course, such relationships rely on the implicit assumption that any future conflicts or disputes can be resolved without a binding document delineating roles, responsibilities, and consequences. If a major conflict or dispute emerges in such a partnership, the parties have nothing more at their disposal to resolve the problem than their own and their partner's flexibility, tolerance, and good will. As we've seen throughout this book, sometimes this is simply not enough.

Committing with a Contract

In contrast to those who are content with just a handshake or a verbal agreement, many people we interviewed based their partnership agreements on formal, legally binding contracts. While the actual development of the contract can often help to clarify roles and obligations before a final commitment is made, most of these people preferred a contract for another reason—security. If the partnership begins to break down at some point, they want a safety valve, which they believe only a contract can offer. As one interviewee told us, "You never regret having a contract in one hand while you're pressing the flesh with the other. Someday, you might hate the contract you signed. But you'll never hate the fact that you had a contract."

Contracts are usually seen as essential in large business alliances.

A typical example is the partnership between Travelers School Services and American Business Services (ABS) to form Urban Food Services. The joint venture was initially agreed to by both Al Demitt of American Business Services and David Sernum, the president of Travelers School Services. But Travelers' legal department insisted that the agreement be formalized in a contract. As the agreement was negotiated, several issues emerged.

The first and perhaps most critical was how profits would be divided. Demitt wanted a 50–50 split. Travelers wanted 75–25, because it would be providing a greater number of resources, or, as we were told, be "bringing more to the party." The final agreement was 65–35, with each organization contributing a corresponding amount toward the initial capital outlay. Another issue was their common concern that ABS (a minority-owned and -run company) would be perceived as simply a front for a large, private, white-owned corporation seeking to enter a market that was actively seeking minority-owned businesses. While no clear answer to this problem was found, let alone included in the contract, both parties agreed in principle to be aware of the possible negative perception and to work hard to present themselves as a true team.

Drafted by Travelers' legal counsel, the final agreement is twenty-nine pages long and is legally binding. It delineates responsibilities, financial arrangements, a process for dissolution, and limitations on growth, by either party, that could jeopardize the venture. In addition, it provides for a management review committee, made up of people from both companies, as the governing board for the venture. In short, it represents a thorough discovery and communication of a basic covenant to work on a collaborative venture toward a goal of mutual gain. In many respects, a contract of this length clearly makes the most sense both for ABS and for Travelers. The joint venture was a complex one, between two partners that had never before worked together. In addition, the negotiating parties, Demitt and Sernum, were not simply representing themselves (as is the case in many smaller partnerships); they were representing their entire organizations, which undoubtedly wanted to have the assurance of a legally binding contract.

What especially intrigued us is how the contract-negotiation process became an occasion for the parties to discuss issues that would not be directly addressed in the contract—issues such as the possible perception of ABS as a Travelers front. Especially among parties that don't know each other well, delicate subjects such as this are often not easy to bring up. In this case, the formal negotiation process helped to create an atmosphere in which this "informal" issue could more easily be discussed in an honest and open way.

Halfway Between Handshake and Contract

Many partnerships we looked at took what we saw as a "middle road" between sole reliance on a handshake and an extensive contract. One of these was the partnership between Ben and Sam, owners of a beer distributorship (Ben) and microbrewery (Sam). Longtime friends, the two took a trip to England together several years ago and spent much of their time in neighborhood pubs, talking about how much fun it would be to have a pub of their own in the United States. After their return, when they were having a drink with two other friends, the conversation came around to the idea of the pub. Soon the four friends realized that, between them, they had just the right mix of expertise needed to begin such a venture. Ben had fourteen years of experience in the food and beverage industry and now owned a distributorship. Sam had been a salesman before starting his microbrewery. And the other two had experience in the construction and hospitality businesses, as well as some investment revenue.

The ultimate decision came when Sam looked over at Ben and simply said, "If you're serious about this, I want in." The four worked for a year and a half to open the Fog and Grog, a neighborhood pub and restaurant. Neither Sam nor Ben abandoned their existing companies; like many people who form partnerships, Sam and Ben formed theirs in order to integrate their existing operations with a newfound interest. The Fog and Grog not only serves some of the gourmet beers and ales Ben distributes, but it is also an outlet for the products of Sam's microbrewery. This joint venture is one of the most successful in the business.

In the beginning, the Fog and Grog was owned equally by the four partners (Ben's and Sam's shares being held by their parent corporations). Their only legal documentation was a standard buy-and-sell agreement. Within six months, however, the partnership was down to just Ben's and Sam's two companies. Conflicts arose as Ben and Sam realized they could not trust the other two as much as they could trust each other to live up to their commitment and meet their responsibilities to the business. So, with the original agreement in hand, Ben's and Sam's organizations bought out the other two parties. Despite these difficult experiences, Ben and Sam did not feel the need to develop an extensive contract with each other. During the crisis, each had come through for the other, and each felt that the other had more than proven that he was trustworthy. With no more than a standard buy-and-sell agreement, the two have remained partners in good standing for the last eight years.

Without any other written agreements or any written policies and procedures, the two have made a concerted effort to create other ways to address problems that might occur. One way, for example, is through weekly meetings. There the two have open discussions of issues that have arisen. There, as Ben told us, they "hash it out until everything is agreeable." Another way is through a unique coping mechanism the two have developed to ensure the health of their partnership, as well as their individual businesses. Because of the nature of their business, both are required to work long hours and both experience a great deal of contact with the public. So, to maintain their sanity, as Sam puts it, they have an unwritten policy that each can leave town for one or two weekends a month with his family and go on an extended holiday for three to four weeks every year, without worrying about their joint venture. Ben and Sam have worked out similar arrangements within their own businesses, so that this time away is truly "renewing." The two partners have even gone so far as to keep an eye on each other's business when the other person is away.

An arrangement structured to assure a high degree of individual autonomy within the bounds of a formal written contract was structured by WorldView Personnel Associates. Based in the Pacific Northwest, this partnership consists of four personnel agencies headed by four women. Rather than a single business, this partnership is more of a joint venture composed of four separate entities. Each partner bills her clients through her own business. Then, together, the four contribute equal amounts of money to the "umbrella firm," as they like to call it, to pay the expenses they share, ranging from office space to clerical help. The four also rotate the role of managing partner (the person responsible for seeing that the common bills are paid and the staff is managed) on a quarterly basis.

Apart from sharing "housekeeping" chores, the four firms have found that their loosely knit partnership offers many additional benefits. While each firm is responsible for its own marketing, the partners often recommend each other for contracts they believe their own firm is not best suited to serve. If one partner's organization has more work than it can handle, she calls on one of her colleagues, giving her firm a chance to pick up additional business. In addition, the four meet often to compare notes, discussing the current business climate in their city, new developments in their industry, and other matters.

With their "umbrella" structure, these four personnel firms remain quite autonomous while also enjoying many of the traditional benefits of partnerships. All four partners are committed to each other; yet, they also remain quite independent. In this case, four people and four organizations have struck a very appealing balance between the isolation and high overhead that can accompany working as autonomous firms and the pervasive, "till death do us part" kind of commitment that can come with a comprehensive, legally binding partnership contract.

Whatever its form, a formal contract can be a valuable asset to a partnership. But, as we heard from partners many times, a contract, while an important tool in a partnership, should never be seen as the sole basis of the partnership. A contract, no matter how "bulletproof," can never be an adequate substitute for trust.

Shake Now, Sign Later

We occasionally found that partners will begin with no more than a handshake and then move to a contract later on, sometimes years after the partnership's formation. While it may be easy to assume that such an action reveals a breakdown in trust, we discovered that, more often than not, something altogether different had happened. Sometimes growing partnerships need a more formal structure, one that it makes sense to define in a detailed written contract. Rather than a response to a lack of trust, these developments are usually a response to success.

One example is HomePaint, a company founded in 1973 by four independent house painters. Initially the four founders shared only a common desire to paint houses. They felt they didn't need a formal, written contract. They had no strategic plan, no organizational vision. They simply shared the burdens of finding customers, completing jobs, and buying supplies on an ad hoc basis. In fact, they even felt there was no need to keep track of their hours. They were all partners, they reasoned, so they would share whatever money they made equally.

Over the years, however, HomePaint went through many changes. Two of the original partners left. Two new partners were brought in. After several years, these two were bought out. By 1981 the partnership had been reduced to two of the original four, Phil and Nelson. These two men, in turn, began their own, independent housepainting businesses, but they have remained as partners and continue to work both independently and together. While the number of partners had been reduced and each partner had established his own business, their joint business had grown. By 1981

Phil and Nelson had forty-five employees between them. It was time, they felt, for a more formal agreement, structure, and division of responsibilities.

Phil and Nelson have put a great deal of time and attention into making sure their employees are competent and content. In fact, they have developed a joint employee training program that has drawn rave reviews from customers. Furthermore, their employees are given a voice in the running of the partnership through elected representatives that sit on the partnership's board of directors. Thus while Phil and Nelson keep rather close control of their own individual companies, they allow and even encourage broad-based ownership of their joint company.

The partnership has changed greatly from its early days, when there was essentially no division of responsibilities. Each partner has gravitated toward roles he feels more comfortable in. Over time, for example, Phil realized that his interest and expertise lay in sales and marketing, while Nelson saw that he prefers to focus more on finance, accounting, and legal issues, as well as on special tasks such as writing a policy manual for the partnership (which was also applicable to both individual companies). In their case, beginning without a contract or even a clear division of labor allowed Phil and Nelson to work in all facets of the business, enabling each of them to eventually start his own company and grow with the business.

In describing their partnership, Phil and Nelson drew an analogy we liked very much. Just as they, the partners, could be compared to a married couple, their partnership could be compared to the "fruit" of their union—it's their child. For them, developing the business was like raising a child, a rewarding experience that can be exhausting as well. Their decision to start their own separate businesses—which brought more structure and discipline to the partnership—can be likened to parents "putting their foot down" to assert authority over an unruly teenager, while also allowing the teenager to become more autonomous and to move out and become more independent. Like conscientious parents, Phil and Nelsen wanted to be in control rather than to be controlled. They responded to this need by starting their own independent businesses and formalizing the rules of their partnership. They also wanted to become more collaborative, however, and they responded to this need by making their partnership more open to employee participation.

While formalizing the commitment after the partnership is well under way can represent progress, it can also be an indicator of potential problems. An interesting example is the unsuccessful health care partnership between Dr. Adams and Dr. Martin that was described in Chapter Five. The story of this troubled partnership began when Dr. Adams observed that the emergency rooms in his community were staffed with residents and staff physicians on a rotating basis. He was concerned on both counts: the residents were often far too inexperienced for this kind of work; and the staff physicians, often specialists in areas such as radiology or orthopedics, were ill equipped to treat patients who had just had a heart attack or a stroke.

Dr. Adams believed that patients are best served when they are treated in a stable environment by physicians with a full-time commitment to emergency medicine. So, as a practicing emergency physician himself, he approached a local hospital and proposed to provide full-time, specialized coverage to the emergency room. Soon he received a call from the hospital's chairman of the board, urging him to sign an agreement.

Since staffing an emergency room requires a great deal of administrative work, Dr. Adams approached a colleague, Dr. Martin, and asked if he would help get the contract started. Dr. Adams would split his time between clinical practice and administrative duties, while Dr. Martin would provide additional clinical support. This was the beginning of their informal partnership. Soon more hospitals wanted this specialized emergency service, and the company quickly began to grow. The partners now had additional responsibilities: developing a fee structure, hiring administrative staff, and overseeing other aspects of the operation.

By 1974 a complex partnership had developed. A family member advised Dr. Martin to enter into a formal partnership. Dr. Adams agreed, documents were signed, and a legally binding partnership was formed. While the decision to formalize an existing partnership was considered a very positive step for the partners in the housepainting businesses, it came as a result of both positive and negative developments for the two doctors. On the positive side, the company was experiencing rapid growth and needed a more formal structure to accommodate continued expansion. Looking back, this was clearly the right move. Today, for example, the company is many times larger than it was then. It has operations in many states, owns and operates several ambulatory care centers, and runs a national physician's billing service.

On the negative side, however, the agreement has helped formalize a "separate but equal" status that both partners seemed to want from the start, given that they didn't know each other well and wanted to preserve their autonomy. Today, for example, Dr. Adams manages major parts of the common enterprise, Dr. Martin oversees the other parts, and very few functions overlap. This explicit separation, we found, has continued because the two men do not get along very well. When they meet to resolve a dispute, for example, the result is usually a heated debate. And their solution has been to make the divisions within the partnership as clear—and complete—as possible, so they can interact as little as possible.

The reasons for this, we believe, can be found in the two doctors' vastly different management styles and perspectives on the business. As mentioned in Chapter Five, Dr. Adams manages in a way that might best be characterized as "collaborative." He encourages personal and professional growth through education and has included educational benefits in the company's employee benefits package. He strongly encourages employees to make decisions, work as teams, and speak up. He even holds regular all-company meetings, which include everyone from the chief operating officer to the mailroom clerk, to update employees on new projects or recent accomplishments. Dr. Martin, on the other hand, is more of a top-down manager. He has only one direct subordinate, his chief of staff, and he interacts very little with the other employees. Needless to say, he has little interest in promoting employee education programs or in asking for feedback.

In this case, a formal, legally binding agreement—perhaps the result of some initial underlying mistrust or discomfort—serves in part to bind two incompatible partners more tightly together in a business that is too successful for either to walk away from. In their own way, they are like the proverbial couple trapped in a loveless marriage, sharing the same house but leading lives that are as separate as possible.

Committing to Partnership

In their 1985 book *Reinventing the Corporation,* John Naisbitt and Patricia Aburdene make a comment we found quite appropriate to the entire process of committing to a partnership. "One of the best-kept secrets in America," they note, "is that people are aching to make a commitment—if they only had the freedom and environment to do so." Certainly this desire has much to do with both the eternal appeal of marriage and the growing appeal of business partnerships. People love the idea of being part of something larger than themselves, and if that something is partially of their own making, then all the better.

But, as our investigation into partnerships confirms, this "aching" desire must also be balanced by equal measures of calm deliberation and sensitivity to the unique facets of the situation. The decision to seal a commitment with a handshake or a comprehensive, legally binding written agreement—or anything in between—depends on many factors: the nature of the relationship between the prospective partners; the values, professional objectives, and personal goals of each partner; the extent to which they share or don't share those values, objectives, and goals; the reasons each has for partnering; and the kind of partnership being formed. While it is a hopeful, sometimes exhilarating, experience, the moment of commitment is also a momentous one, requiring the utmost care and consideration. Not only is an agreement being made, but so is a covenant.

Chapter Ten

Building a Foundation for Mutual Trust

We began preparing for this book by reading all that was available about partnerships and by discussing and distilling our own experiences in consulting to, forming, and working in various partnership arrangements. Some of our initial impressions held up well as we began to place our findings down on paper. In many instances, however, we were either surprised by or particularly intrigued with unexpected or unique experiences and insights offered by the people we interviewed. We have tried to make some sense of these more maverick findings. We have also moved beyond our initial analyses in reflecting back on our results. But a difficult question was inevitably posed: So what? What can be done to tangibly improve the chances of making a correct decision regarding a new partnership? What about entering an existing partnership? And how does one effectively manage a partnership that is already under way?

We turn in this final chapter to our findings and to our reflections on these findings. We propose several specific tools that might be used to address these "so what" questions. Specifically, we focus on three central lessons we have learned concerning the problem-solving basis of partnerships and the central role played by trust in partnerships.

First, we learned that partnerships are often formed after some major problem or challenge has been identified that could not be solved through the regular mechanisms of the existing organizations. Second, we discovered that, while it is abundantly clear that people consider partnership for a wide variety of reasons, they almost always become partners for a combination of reasons.

Third, the issue of trust was identified as particularly important in the formation and maintenance of partnerships. Trust in intentions centers on partners' assessment of the other partners' sense of honor and commitment. This commitment, in turn, is directly relevant to the continuation and nurturance of the partnership. Trust in competency is important to the extent that there is specialization of functions within the partnership. We found that three factors are critical with regard to competency: capacity, accessibility, and dependability. Finally, trust based on a shared perspective is most often the result of complementary—rather than identical—attitudes regarding the business the partners are in together. The extent to which the partners' perspectives should be complementary rather than identical depends on how important shared goals are to the partnership, the nature and extent of the partners' past partnership experiences, and the extent to which there is support in the partnership for resolving conflict and disagreements.

In this concluding chapter we expand upon these three major lessons and illustrate them by returning one last time to our interviews and our three case studies.

Deciding Whether or Not to Form a Partnership

We initially suggested in Chapter Three that there are three overriding motives for starting a partnership: pragmatism, personal fulfillment, and enjoyment of the partnership experience. Results from our case study analyses certainly support the important role played by these motives. Several other general findings, however, emerged from our further assessment of partnerships.

Partnerships are often formed after some major problem or challenge has been identified that the participants cannot readily solve on their own. Thus, the pragmatism motive we identified in Chapter Three appears to be particularly important, though it may be based not so much on how the partnership will benefit the participating companies in general as on how it will enable each company to better tackle a specific problem the companies all face.

We also found, however, that partnerships are often self-replicating. Having initially formed a partnership to address a specific, pressing problem, partners often go on to pursue whole new endeavors, equipping themselves to venture forth to create new products and services and to tap new markets. Successful partnerships seem to breed additional partnerships. It was the Norpac leaders' experience and expertise in the formation of the Norpac partnership itself, for instance, that made them willing to enter into another innovative and risky partnership with Lesher Communications. It was because of the many partnerships that Arthur Andersen had formed with other organizations that the leaders of the firm were able to move confidently and persuasively into a partnership with the Alameda school system. Various partnerships that had already been formed among the highly competitive businesses of Silicon Valley set the stage for and softened opposition to the formation of a new form of partnership through the Council for Continuous Improvement. When people create partnerships, they also create an atmosphere conducive to the creation of other partnerships and participation in other modes of cooperation—particularly if their first partnership is successful.

Our interviews and case studies clearly indicate that partnerships are rarely founded because they are more fun than going it alone—although after they are formed, partnerships often become a rich source of gratification for all involved and may create a desire to forge additional partnerships. Usually partnerships emerge from the necessity for change and from pressure either from the external environment or from farsighted leaders within an organization who somehow sense that things can't stay like they are. Thus, partnerships of function are common in the early stages, whereas partnerships of commitment tend to emerge later and often spawn other partnerships.

Given the central role played by pragmatism or, more specifically, the resolution of an immediate problem, what kind of questions should be asked when deciding whether or not to start a partnership? Ironically, we think that it is particularly important to move beyond pragmatic concerns when deciding on forming a partnership. We recommend a broader perspective, precisely because of the temptation to form a partnership simply to solve a specific problem. We recommend this because we not only found that partnerships often begin as an attempt to solve a pressing problem, we also found that many failed partnerships began precisely for this same short-term reason, and as a result were never solidly based. While short-term partnerships (for example, consultative relationships) may at times be appropriate (as in the case of the Catholic church parish and the fundraiser), longer-term partnerships should only be formed when there is at least the prospect of broader benefits.

What then are the key questions one should ask about one's own motivation and the motivation of potential partners with regard to forming a partnership? In identifying these key questions, we looked not only at the three motives but also the six reasons for partnership that we identified in the first chapter of this book, for both the three motives and the six reasons were frequently revealed in our study of partnerships. We have summarized the outcome of our analyses in the Partnership Readiness Questionnaire reprinted in the appendix to this book. We suggest that you review this list when considering forming a partnership.

More specifically, we suggest that you fill out this questionnaire to get a sense of your organization's readiness for partnership, and we suggest that you also give this questionnaire to other members of your organization to check out your own perceptions of the current conditions in your organization. Don't just rely on your own judgment. When you have completed this brief survey, add up your score. Typically, a score of 30 or more suggests that a partnership will make sense for your organization. Scores under 20 suggest that your organization should be very cautious in considering the formation of a partnership. If your score lies between 20 and 30, look at the sources of your high and low scores.

If the pragmatic scores tend to be high (4's and 5's) then your organization may want to move ahead with the partnership, given that the more personal factors are likely to increase once the partnership begins (as was so evident in the Lesher-Norpac partnership). If the pragmatism scores are low (3 and under) then your organization might want to hold up on partnering. Even if a partnership "feels" like a good idea (satisfying the personal-fulfillment criterion), it has to "make sense" (satisfying the pragmatism criterion) if it is to work. Concentrate on building up the pragmatic benefits before initiating a partnership that is merely personally desirable.

While it's abundantly clear that people consider partnership for a wide variety of reasons, we want to emphasize that people almost always become partners for a *combination* of reasons. That's why we suggest that you rate your organization on all eight of the items on the Partnership Readiness Questionnaire and add up the eight scores to obtain a single overall score. Rarely, if ever, does an organization seek a partner only to serve one narrow purpose or to satisfy one narrow need.

The alliance between BiChip and TechnoCorp, for instance, was not created simply because BiChip needed TechnoCorp's start-up dollars and office space. If this were the case, then BiChip would score a 5 on the fourth item ("resources"), but not on the other seven. The engineers at BiChip wanted to play a hands-on role in developing a product of their very own. They were in search of greater professional and, ultimately, personal fulfillment (items 7 and 8). Likewise, Marilyn and Kathleen, the heads of two very prosperous management and career-development consulting firms, have not allied themselves with each other merely because they enjoy working together (item 8). Each brings complementary talent and expertise from their own individual firm to the common enterprise—qualities that fill in the gaps and, in doing so, enhance the service they provide to their clients (items 2 and 4).

We found that the smaller the partnership, the larger the number of complementary resources a prospective partner may be required to bring to the alliance. In a joint venture between two small consulting firms, for example, each party might have to contribute a bit of everything: some of the money, some of the marketing know-how, some of the technical expertise, and some of the "grunt work."

Whether small organizations or very large organizations are involved, the process of considering partnership usually turns out to be much more complex than it initially seems. Not only must all prospective partners assess why they want to enter into this kind of arrangement, but they must also assess what they can bring to it and what they need most from their potential partners. They should all fill out the Partnership Readiness Questionnaire with each of their prospective partners to determine whether or not they have sufficiently good reasons for entering the partnership. Needless to say, the choice of a specific partner or partners can be just as important and complex as the decision to enter into a partnership in the first place. The selection of partners involves an assessment of each potential partner's strengths and shortcomings and an assessment of how they mesh with one another.

Our interviews also revealed that an additional factor must be considered if the partnership is to move beyond function to commitment. Those who are participating in a partnership of commitment should share a sense of direction and purpose for the partnership. In his discussion of the new "learning organization," Peter Senge (1990) emphasizes the roles of vision and values. Contemporary organizations, according to Senge, will survive and thrive only if they are clear about their mission and purpose. Whereas premodern organizations' missions were typically an inherent part of the work they performed (usually agricultural or craft-based) and modern organizations could be concerned primarily with expansion and growth while ignoring their mission and purpose, contemporary, postmodern organizations must be clear about the direction in which they intend to move.

Given that most postmodern organizations—and partnerships in particular—have very unclear boundaries, a clear mission and a firm commitment to partnership is needed to keep the organization from flying apart. It is clear from our interviews that a partnership's mission and values are intimately intertwined with the partners' mutual commitment. A partnership's mission and vision help define the nature and scope of the partners' commitment, and their commitment to the partnership in turn provides energy and structure for ensuring an enduring focus on its mission and vision. In many respects, the mutual commitment *is* the mission and the vision. Furthermore, given the necessity to continually assess the shifting needs of their customers, postmodern partnerships must be established on the basis of a shared commitment to and orientation toward the customer, while also satisfying the needs of the partners.

Many of our subjects spoke of the critical importance of their partnership's mutual commitment and mission, or they spoke of their fears and concerns regarding either not having a commitment or a clear mission statement or having a partnership agreement or mission statement that is now out-of-date.

The mission at BiChip and TechnoCorp, right from the start, was to deliver the first product. Both parties were committed to the partnership because it met several independent needs of each party. It is now time, as the president of BiChip notes, to revise and elevate the partnership's commitment and mission, given that BiChip and TechnoCorp successfully delivered their first product. The new commitment and mission must support the journey the partnership is beginning on the open market. BiChip's president spoke poignantly on the subject for a few minutes, acknowledging that he didn't have a good idea as to what the revised commitment and mission should be, but he also acknowledged that the company could get into trouble quickly without one. He felt that BiChip was floating a bit, now that the founding goals were accomplished. Like many partnerships that are formed with and benefit from considerable flexibility and pragmatism, there is a tendency to be too flexible and too oriented to the moment, resulting eventually in a sense of aimlessness. It is critical for partners to be clear about their commitment and purpose if their flexibility and pragmatism are to remain an asset rather than becoming a source of organizational dysfunction.

Building Trust into the Partnership

Most partnerships begin with personal relationships. Someone knows someone else and talks with that person about forming a partnership. Unlike stock offerings or even the formation of a non-profit board of directors, partnerships are usually formed between people who know each other and may even have worked together. At the very least, partnerships are usually formed between people who have been brought together by a trusted third party.

This interpersonal ingredient—which, as we have seen, is central to all stages of a successful partnership—is crucial for several reasons. People and organizations forming a partnership confront a difficult problem: they need to work with someone they can trust. Trust is so critical because partnerships are more intimate than virtually any other form of organization. Partners must rely on each other completely.

In Chapter Three we identified three different areas in which partners must trust one another: intentions, competency, and perspectives. Our case studies revealed that trust in one's partner in all three of these areas is essential for a successful partnership. Following are some of our reflections on what our case studies revealed about these three spheres of trust.

Intentions

Once we begin to focus on another person's intentions, we have clearly moved into the realm of a very traditional (and not very modern) notion about business-related relationships—the notion that attention must be paid first and foremost to the other person's sense of honor and commitment. As we have suggested throughout this book, many successful partnerships have established a level of commitment between two or more partners that moves well beyond the functional level. There is a deep commitment, based on shared values, that cannot easily be abrogated by either party. This trust in one's partners' intentions ultimately seems to stem from a recognized mutual commitment to the continuation and nurturance of the partnership. This commitment unifies the partnership and ensures that the partners share a common interest in the welfare of the organization. What, concretely, does this mutual commitment look like when two or more organizations are considering a partnership? Our research suggests that two major criteria are critical: the commitment to continuation and the commitment to nurturance.

Commitment to Continuation

- All partners agree to give the partnership an appropriate and agreed-upon period of time to build before any consideration is given to its discontinuation. This period of time extends beyond the duration of the bailout clause in a typical cooperative agreement between independent organizations.

- All partners agree to identify and confront all disagreements and conflicts immediately and to devote substantial time, resources, and personal effort to the resolution or at least management of all conflicts, on behalf of the partnership's continuation.

Commitment to Nurturance

- All partners agree to give the partnership's enterprises their consistent and thoughtful attention and to consider themselves fully accountable (along with the other partners) for the relative success or failure of the enterprises and the partnership.

- All partners will provide appropriate and sufficient resources and attention to this partnership in order to maximize its chances of success, growth, maturation and continuation.

Let's turn to an actual partnership to see how these criteria hold up and play out. In this instance, we will look to a partnership that has not been successful. Ted owns a company that buys up scrap metal and transforms it into high-quality materials. He has been quite successful over the past five years. Not only can he save money for other companies while providing high-quality materials for them to use, but his company also effectively addresses environmental implications by recycling scrap metal. Isamu owns a company that builds highly durable goods—notably the encasements for high-tech equipment such as large computerized control systems. Ted and Isamu had some initial success in establishing a partnership. Ted's company became the sole-source provider of sheet metal for Isamu's company, and Isamu's company became involved in the redesign of production processes at Ted's company to ensure consistent high quality in the sheet metal it produced. In many ways, this partnership held the same potential as that formed between Lesher Communications and Norpac.

However, Ted and Isamu never seemed to develop a shared vision of what they wanted the new product—the sheet metal—to be. Ted was inclined to emphasize low costs, while Isamu was committed to high quality. In commenting on his failed partnership, Ted refers to the Buddhist ideal for partnerships—*itai doshin* (a Japanese phrase meaning "many in body, one in mind")—suggesting that if a partnership is of one mind, then it will succeed. Ted felt that he and Isamu were instead practicing *dotai ishin* ("one in body, many in mind"), and the mediocre performance of their joint business was the predictable result. Ted sees the ingredients for having "one mind"—mutual trust in intentions—as a common vision, compatible styles, and synchronous rules and expectations from the beginning of the partnership. Ted notes that even if two people start out with "one mind," there is a need for continuous monitoring and mechanisms to ensure that there is no divergence of purpose.

If we look at this partnership through the lenses of our criteria, several qualities immediately emerge. First, a state of *itai doshin* implies a strong commitment both to continuation and nurturance. Specifically, Ted felt that neither he nor Isamu ever gave the partnership sufficient attention. For both of them, the new joint venture was always a secondary endeavor. When in doubt, both men—and the people who worked for them—set aside their new venture in favor of the ongoing operations and problems of their own companies. Because of their failures to come together in a shared vision, the partnership between Ted's and Isamu's companies always played second fiddle. They were never committed to the ongoing nurturance of the partnership. Like a neglected child, the partnership simply withered away—and damaged those employees in both companies who made a personal investment in this new joint venture.

As Ted noted, their problems were also exacerbated by different management styles. Ted's organization was very production-oriented and quite formal in terms of hierarchy. By contrast, Isamu operated in a much more relaxed manner and invited active participation by his employees in the design of new products. Ironically, Ted had been intrigued about working with Isamu and his company precisely because of this more collaborative style and their emphasis on quality. Ted's interests in Japanese management theory led him (perhaps unwisely) into this partnership. Yet once the partnership had been formed, this style became a constant irritant for Ted. Furthermore, neither Ted nor Isamu was willing to confront their difference (which is a key ingredient in a commitment to continuation).

Finally, Ted notes a lack of clear rules and expectations, which often results from or helps to produce mistrust regarding partners' intentions. Ted expected Isamu to release four design engineers full-time for the new venture. Isamu believes that he only agreed to supply four half-time engineers (or two full-time engineers). Ted also assumed that Isamu was going to put much more money into the new venture than he did during the first year. Isamu assumed it would be a much slower start-up. Ted originally believed that *itai doshin* means informality and reliance on implicit (unspoken) rather than explicit (publicly articulated) rules and expectations. He eventually learned that this is not the case—an expensive lesson.

So how does one concretely determine another's intentions? Typically, the most important factors leading to trust in intentions concern the sharing of norms and values. While the skills and experiences of successful partners are often complementary rather than similar, comparable norms and values are usually crucial. The men and women we interviewed consistently indicated, through their words or their shared experiences, that partners must share norms and values.

Shared norms and values certainly served as an underpinning for the Lesher-Norpac partnership, as well as the partnership between Arthur Andersen and the Alameda school system. Lesher's and Norpac's leaders were all committed not only to greater levels of collaboration between themselves, but also to greater participation on the part of their employees in the decision-making and problem-solving processes of their respective businesses. Similarly, Arthur Andersen and Alameda were jointly committed to a distinctive vision of what an educational experience could be for children. Even in the case of a loosely configured partnership like CCI, there are certain shared norms and values—at CCI there is the commitment to improved processes for assessing and maintaining product quality.

Let's return to one of the successful partnerships we studied in this book to see how this factor of shared norms and values plays out. Marilyn and Kathleen have established what they call an "alliance of the heart," through which they have joined together two prospering consulting firms to provide management and career-development services to a variety of corporations in the United States. Marilyn and Kathleen created their partnership twelve years ago. No formal letters of agreement or contractual arrangements have been established between their consulting firms. Their mutual commitment seems to be built instead on several clearly articulated statements of philosophy and value.

First of all, they greatly value both collaboration and independence. They pool their resources, yet often their two independent consulting firms work independently of one another. While each firm works extensively with many other consulting firms and independent contractors in various loosely formed and temporary partnerships, they always return to their commitment to this particular partnership, and they look to this long-term partnership for stability and professional development. When Marilyn and Kathleen have the opportunity to personally work together, it is often to learn new techniques and skills from one another—particularly given Marilyn's expertise in career development and Kathleen's expertise in systems change. Other staff members from both firms also learn from their compatriots in the other firm.

Second, both Marilyn and Kathleen—as well as their staffs—value open communication and the establishment of absolute trust. While they have conflicts, they "walk and talk and get it out. It never lingers overnight," according to Marilyn. "We may fight about perspectives, have different judgments around use of products—do we have or do we need to design something?—" Kathleen notes, "but there is never a difference over roles, loyalty, or control." Their partnership is anchored in an unshakable trust and respect for each other's abilities (a melding of trust in intention with trust in competence).

Third, Kathleen and Marilyn value longevity and long-term commitment to relationships. With longevity has come understanding and knowledge. According to Marilyn, "There are many times when we literally finish each other's sentences. We know what's in each other's heads. There have been occasions when we have had such a positive . . . interaction, we could have flown the plane home [from a consultation] ourselves." Because of their commitment to the long-term relationship between their consulting firms, Marilyn and Kathleen have also been there for each other during times of personal crisis. In essence, both women value what Deborah Tannen (1990) calls "rapport talk," as well as the more male-oriented "report talk." They intermix personal and business-related conversations and easily shift between personal and professional concerns. In this emphasis on conversation, flexibility, trust, and commitment, Marilyn and Kathleen demonstrate rather than just declare that "the center will hold" in their partnership—a partnership based on shared values, a partnership of the heart.

Finally, both women share a commitment to furthering the careers of other women, especially women who have experienced racism and discrimination. Many of the conflicts that might otherwise be experienced by Kathleen and Marilyn can be set aside when they consider their mutual commitment to a community goal that supersedes their own personal problems and disagreements.

Competency

Our case studies revealed that trust in the competency of one's partners is particularly important if there is a specialization of functions within the partnership. If you choose to partner with another person because he or she knows something or can do something that you can't do or don't know how to do, then it is critical that you have full confidence in that person's ability to employ these skills and use this knowledge in the partnership. By competency we mean not only knowledge and skills, but also the capacity of the partner organization to provide other resources and markets and to be flexible and cooperative.

What factors should define how important competency is in the selection of specific partners? Our research suggests that three factors are critical:

1. Capacity. Does the prospective partner have the resources, markets, and/or skills of flexibility and cooperation that my organization needs (as identified by the Partnership Readiness Questionnaire)?
2. Accessibility. Is the prospective partner willing and/or able to make these resources, markets, and/or skills available to the partnership?

3. Dependability. Are the needed capacities of this prospective partner likely to be available only in the short-term? Is their availability likely to fluctuate over time? Or are they likely to be long-term and enduring?

Once again, let's return to one set of partnership interviews to see how these three factors play out. In commenting on Bay Electronics's four-year-old high-tech partnership with General Systech, Sid observes that as leader and owner of Bay Electronics he has come to know and trust the president of General Systech, Bertrand Weiss. The two of them have grown to know each other at a much deeper level and feel increasingly comfortable with each other's skills as leaders of companies operating in a highly turbulent business environment. This comfort level allows their companies to work more autonomously in their respective areas of competency, because each company and its staff "knows" that its partner company is competent in fulfilling certain production roles. But what factors led to this trust in each partner's competency? First, let's look at the partners' capacity. When these two companies first came together, they knew little about each other's intentions, but they did know quite a bit about each other's strengths and weaknesses. Bay Electronics is particularly adept at producing custom-designed electronic equipment for single customers, while General Systech is noted for production of low-cost, high-volume electronic equipment. Thus, they fulfilled the first requirement of trust in competency—namely, capacity.

The second ingredient—accessibility—was also present. The leaders of Bay Electronics knew that their company could make use of General Systech's low-cost, high-quality products when its custom-made equipment could incorporate these products, while the leaders of General Systech knew that they could make use of Bay Electronics when one of its customers needed to modify one of General Systech's products for a special use.

Finally, let's look at dependability. Sid and Bertrand have come to understand clearly the roles and responsibilities that each company plays with regard to the partnership. They both are confident that they are operating with both businesses' best interests at heart (a combination of trust in competence and trust in intentions). They can divide and conquer. They do not have to do everything together, and they can form other partnerships without raising either jealousy or suspicion. Sid feels this is a very positive aspect of their partnership. It helps to ensure continued access (the second factor) and dependability (the third factor).

Through our case studies, we discovered another important lesson regarding trust in competency: while partners' norms and values should be similar in order to establish mutual trust in their intentions, different and complementary skills between partners promote a trust in their respective competency. Let's see what this looks like through another set of interviews. SHOWCO is a partnership between two large ticketing agencies. The owner of one of these firms, Ben Davitz indicated that SHOWCO has been very successful because both partners built on the distinctive strengths of the other partner's agency. As Ben stated, "My talent and interest is with the people—promotion and marketing. Merv's is research-oriented. . . . It became very apparent that between us, we'd make the perfect team." Merv agreed: "We both respect what the other can do. Ben has that marvelous talent for communicating the philosophy of what we're doing and why." SHOWCO is a partnership based on the successful meshing of different skills. "We egg each other on," recalls Merv, "but over the years, we've learned from each other."

In this instance, there was always an appreciation of the partners' differences in skills. This was essential when the partnership was formed; as the business evolved, each partner learned from the other and became able to do many of the things that were originally part of the other partner's area of specialization. Other partners talk about going through an early stage of major differentiation in functions and skills and a later merger as the business became larger and more complex and the partners began to hire other staff members with specific expertise and skills. This represents a shift from a partnership of function to a partnership of commitment.

Perspectives

While most partners would agree that successful partners tend to share common values and complementary skills, there is less agreement when it comes to a third dimension—namely, the perspectives one has on business and, more generally, on relationships with other people and on life in general. Some of the people we interviewed indicate that partners should share common attitudes and look at life in a similar manner. For many others, however, it seems to be important that partners share complementary—rather than identical—attitudes. This sometimes means that one of the partners is very patient and tends to look at the long-term picture, while the other partner is more impatient and oriented toward the short-term benefits of the organization. Both perspectives are essential, and the loss of either one can be disastrous for an organization. Perhaps CCI needs such a corrective, given Reilly's strong commitment to growth and expansion of mission and partnership. Should Pete Hamm, the successor to Reilly at CCI, be the person who asks why the partnership is growing and what will be lost with an expansion in its scope and mission?

What factors should determine if a partnership should be constituted of people and organizations with identical perspectives or with similar but complementary perspectives? Three factors are critical in making this decision:

1. A shared goal

   Is the partnership being formed to further some important cause, or is it based on a shared vision of some desired state of affairs? If it is, then a close match in perspectives is critical.

   Is the partnership being formed to further the individual

goals of each partner organization, rather than a shared goal? If it is, then slight differences in perspectives may benefit the overall success of the partners.

2. Past experience in partnerships

Is this one of the first times these organizations have participated in a partnership? If it is, then close alignment of perspectives is desirable.

Have these organizations (and their leaders) participated in many other partnerships—with some degree of success? If so, then these partners may be able to work easily with and benefit from differing perspectives.

3. Support for resolving conflict and disagreements

Is the climate in each organization supportive of airing conflict and open disagreement, and are the key staff who are likely to participate in the partnership skillful in managing conflict and disagreement? If so, differences in perspective are appropriate and potentially beneficial.

Does the climate in each organization tend to discourage conflict and the open display of disagreement, and are key members of the staff not particularly skillful in managing conflict? If so, then identical or very similar perspectives are critical.

These three factors came into play when two particular organizations—restaurants located next door to each other—were considering forming a partnership several years ago. The owners felt that a partnership would enable them to share certain kitchen facilities and even staff, as one restaurant is open only for breakfast and the other only for lunch and dinner.

When the two owners sat together, it became clear that one of them, Mark, was more patient and oriented toward the long-term future of his restaurant. He was much more interested in remaining with the business over the long haul than was Gigi, owner of the second restaurant. Gigi indicated that, although she finds it very exciting to start a business, she feels that a business can become so consuming that at some point she may want to be free of it. Thus she tends to take a short-term, profit-oriented approach to her restaurant. Furthermore, she doesn't think that partnerships are forever. Eventually, any partnership probably will dissolve and the partners will go their separate ways.

According to Gigi, if the partnership were to become particularly difficult for one or both parties, then it would need to be dissolved without anyone being hurt. She acknowledged that this usually doesn't occur. There are often terrible fights, and someone comes out on the losing end. And Gigi seemed to feel the need for a private life more than ever before in her life. Mark didn't seem to be as much in need of such limits; he wanted as much involvement as possible. Thus Mark was interested in shaping the future of his restaurant around a partnership with Gigi's restaurant, while Gigi wanted to place some boundaries around the partnership so that it didn't get out of hand.

Mark and Gigi wanted to know what to do. They applied the three criteria on our list. First, did they share a common goal? While both were in the restaurant business and were interested in preparing excellent food, they didn't share an overarching goal or mission—as might two restaurant owners trying to create a "restaurant row" in their community. Given, then, that the partnership wouldn't have been formed around a shared goal, a difference in perspective might have been perfectly acceptable. Second, did either of them have much experience in managing previous partnerships? In this instance, partnering would have been a totally new experience for both Mark and Gigi—suggesting that they would need to have closely aligned perspectives on their businesses.

Third, what about their ability to manage conflict? As we sat down and discussed this matter, Mark indicated that he generally tries to avoid conflict at all costs, while Gigi said that she readily leaps into conflicts, tends to shrug off disagreements, and rarely holds grudges. This difference in style suggested that these two would not easily manage their conflicts, hence they should form a partnership only if they had very compatible perspectives.

What kind of conclusion was reached? We suggested that they not form this partnership. The combination of Mark's long-term perspective and Gigi's short-term perspective could be quite valuable, if the two of them had been experienced in building a partnership and in managing the inevitable conflicts. However, in this case, one could anticipate that the two organizations would often be bumping up against each other and that the partnership could be a burden rather than a benefit to both parties. Mark would have been looking toward the long-term benefits of the partnership and would likely have invested more resources and attention in the partnership than Gigi would have. She would have been more interested in the short-term payoffs and probably would have been less willing to invest in the partnership for the long-term. Both Mark and Gigi agreed with this analysis and decided to back away from the partnership—though since that time they have cautiously begun to explore several less ambitious modes of cooperation (regarding advertising and purchasing of food in greater bulk).

Building Strategic Relationships

At one point in Ernest Hemingway's novel *The Sun Also Rises*, the hero-narrator, Jake Barnes, makes a remark about his world that many of today's new and potential partners might easily make about theirs: "I didn't know what it was all about. All I wanted to know was how to live in it." Today, there's little doubt that strategic relationships are already critical to people working not only in business but also in government, education, nonprofit groups—organizations of virtually every kind. There's little doubt that their importance is increasing. And there's little doubt that, while they offer enormous new opportunities, they are rarely, if ever, easy.

The inevitable question then becomes "How can I seek out,

create, and maintain successful strategic relationships?" Although we cannot fully answer this question for you, we hope that this book—filled with the candid words of participants in real-life partnerships—has offered the kinds of insights that can help you answer it for yourself.

Resource

Partnership Readiness Questionnaire

Rate each of the eight items listed using the following five-point scale as a guideline. Place the appropriate number from this scale in the space located to the left of each item. Obtain a total readiness score by adding together your eight ratings.

Five-point scale:

5 = *Strongly agree.* This statement very accurately describes the state of my organization and/or my own beliefs and attitudes.

4 = *Moderately agree.* This statement is fairly accurate in describing the state of my organization and/or my own beliefs and attitudes.

3 = *Indeterminate.* This statement is unrelated to the state of my organization or my own beliefs and attitudes, or I am unable to make a determination with regard to this factor.

2 = *Moderately disagree.* This statement is fairly inaccurate in describing the state of my organization and/or my own beliefs and attitudes.

1 = *Strongly disagree.* This statement is very inaccurate in describing the state of my organization and/or my own beliefs and attitudes.

I. Pragmatism

___ 1. *Efficiency: Cost.* Our product or service could be offered at a lower cost if we were able to combine efforts with one or more organizations.

___ 2. *Efficiency: Quality.* Our product or service could be offered at a higher quality (but not a higher cost) if we were able to combine efforts with one or more organizations.

___ 3. *Flexibility.* Our organization could more readily shift and adjust its structures or processes to meet changing and/or unpredictable needs and conditions if we were able to combine efforts with one or more organizations.

___ 4. *Resources.* Our organization needs resources that we do not now possess in sufficient quantity or quality and that we either cannot afford at all or need on a full-time basis. These resources are available in one or more other organizations.

___ 5. *Expanded Markets.* Our organization can benefit from making its products or services available in a new geographical region or to a new segment of the population we currently serve by cooperating with one or more organizations that do have access to this region or population segment.

II. Personal Fulfillment

___ 6. *Flexibility.* My own job and/or the jobs of many people in this organization would become easier to manage and more adaptable to changing or unpredictable needs and conditions if our organization were to cooperate with one or more organizations.

___ 7. *Personal Gratification.* Other members of this organization and/or I would become much more involved in, have more control over, and/or be more satisfied with the work environment if our organization were to enter into a cooperative agreement with one or more organizations.

III. *Enjoying the Partnership Experience*

___ 8. *Personal Gratification*. I believe that other members of this organization and/or I would find a partnership with one or more organizations a source of challenge, excitement, personal learning, and/or professional development.

___ *Total Score* (Add scores for items 1–8)

References

Argyris, C. *Reasoning, Learning, and Action: Individual and Organizational*. San Francisco: Jossey-Bass, 1982.

Argryis, C., and Schön, D. A. *Organizational Learning: A Theory of Action Perspective*. Reading, Mass.: Addison-Wesley, 1978.

Atchison, S. "Grand Ole Symphony?" *Business Week*, Sept. 6, 1993, pp. 76–78.

Bellah, R., and others. *Habits of the Heart*. Berkeley: University of California Press, 1985.

Bellah, R., and others. *The Good Society*. New York: Knopf, 1991.

Bergquist, W. *The Postmodern Organization: Mastering the Art of Irreversible Change*. San Francisco: Jossey-Bass, 1993.

Bergquist, W., and Weiss, B. *Freedom: Narratives of Change in Hungary and Estonia*. San Francisco: Jossey-Bass, 1994.

Bleeke J., and Ernst, D. "The Way to Win in Cross-Border Alliances." *Harvard Business Review*, Nov.-Dec. 1991, p. 127.

Block, P. *Stewardship: Choosing Service over Self Interest*. San Francisco: Berrett-Koehler, 1993.

Boulding, K. "Intersects: The Peculiar Organizations." In K. Bursk (ed.), *Challenge to Leadership: Managing in a Changing World*. New York: Free Press, 1973.

Brodkin, M. *Every Kid Counts: 31 Ways to Save Our Children*. San Francisco: HarperCollins, 1993.

Byrne, J., Brandt, R., and Port, O. "The Virtual Corporation." *Business Week*, Feb. 8, 1993, p. 100.

Carter, J. *Talking Peace: A Vision for the Next Generation*. New York: Dutton, 1993.

Colman, A., and Bexton, W. H. (eds.). *Group Relations Reader*. Anchorage, Ky.: GREX Press, 1975.

Csikszentmihalyi, M. *Beyond Boredom and Anxiety: The Experience of Play in Work and Games*. San Francisco: Jossey-Bass, 1975.

Csikszentmihalyi, M. *Flow: The Psychology of Optimal Experience*. New York: HarperCollins, 1990.

Del Prado, Y., and others. *Tandem: Leadership Through Partnership*. Cupertino, Calif.: Tandem Computers, 1992.

Drucker, P. *The New Realities*. New York: HarperCollins, 1989.

Durkheim, E. *The Division of Labor in Society*. New York: Free Press, 1933. (Originally published 1893.)

Dusharme, D. "Education and Industry Partner for Quality." *Quality Digest*, Feb. 1994, p.12.

Eisler, R. *The Chalice and the Blade*. San Francisco: HarperCollins, 1987.

Flagg, L. "The 'Virtual Enterprise': Your New Model for Success." *Electronic Business*, Mar. 30, 1992.

Gilligan, C. *In a Different Voice*. Cambridge, Mass.: Harvard University Press, 1982.

Hamel, G., Doz, Y., and Prahalad, C. "Collaborate with Your Competitors—and Win." *Harvard Business Review*, Jan.-Feb. 1989, p. 138.

Hardesty, S., and Jacobs, N. *Success and Betrayal: The Crisis of Women in Corporate America*. New York: Franklin Watts, 1986.

"Industry-Academe Bond Strengthens." *Quality*, Feb. 1994, p. 9.

Jameson, F. *Postmodernism or the Cultural Logic of Late Capitalism*. Durham, N.C.: Duke University Press, 1991.

Jewett, J. "How These Firms Made Their Vendors Partners in Success." *Communications News*, 1991, 28(6), 54.

Jick, T. "Customer-Supplier Partnerships: Human Resources as Bridge Builders." *Human Resource Management*, 1990, 29(4), 435–454.

Joba, C., Maynard, H. B., Jr., and Ray, M. "Competition, Cooperation, and Co-Creation: Insights from the World Business Academy." In M. Ray and A. Rinzler (eds.), *The New Paradigm in Business*. New York: Putnam, 1993.

Kanter, R. "Collaborative Advantage." *Harvard Business Review*, July-Aug. 1994, pp. 96–108.

Lawrence, P., and Lorsch, J. *Organization and Environment*. Cambridge, Mass.: Harvard Business School, 1967.

Lawler, E. E., III. *High-Involvement Management: Participative Strategies for Improving Organizational Performance*. San Francisco: Jossey-Bass, 1986.

Lawler, E. E., III. *The Ultimate Advantage: Creating the High-Involvement Organization*. San Francisco: Jossey-Bass, 1992.

Lei, D., and Slocum, J. "Global Strategic Alliances: Payoffs and Pitfalls." *Organizational Dynamics*, Winter 1991, p. 44.

Mamis, R. "Partner Wars: Six True Confessions." *Inc.*, July 1994, pp. 36 ff.

Marrow, A. *Practical Theorist: The Life and Work of Kurt Lewin*. New York: Basic Books, 1969.

Martin, R. "Allied Power." *Horizon Air Magazine*, June 1994, pp. 22–32.

Meyer M. "Here's a 'Virtual' Model for America's Industrial Giants." *Newsweek*, Aug. 23, 1993, p. 40.

Naisbitt, J. *Megatrends*. New York: Warner Books, 1984.

Naisbitt, J., and Aburdene, P. *Reinventing the Corporation*. New York: Warner Books, 1985.

Nanda, A., and Bartlett, C. "Corning Incorporated: A Network of Alliances." In C. Bartlett and S. Goshal (eds.), *Transnational Management: Text, Cases and Readings*. Homewood, Ill.: Irwin, 1991.

Nauss, D. "U.S. to Help Big 3 Make 'Clean Car.'" *San Francisco Chronicle*, Sept. 20, 1993, pp. 1, 13.

Perry. W. *Forms of Intellectual and Ethical Development in the College Years: A Scheme*. Fort Worth: Holt, Rinehart and Winston, 1970.

Ray, M., and Rinzler, A. (eds.). *The New Paradigm in Business*. New York: Putnam, 1993.

Satir, V. *Peoplemaking*. Palo Alto, Calif.: Science and Behavior Books, 1972.

Sarason, S. B. *The Creation of Settings and the Future Societies*. San Francisco: Jossey-Bass, 1972.

Schein, E. H. *Organizational Culture and Leadership: A Dynamic View*. San Francisco: Jossey-Bass, 1985.

Schön, D. A. *The Reflective Practitioner: How Professionals Think in Action*. New York: Basic Books, 1983.

Senge, P. *The Fifth Discipline*. New York: Doubleday, 1990.

Sennett, R. *Authority*. New York: Random House, 1981.

Silver, N. "Volunteerism in Community Agencies." Unpublished doctoral dissertation, Professional School of Psychology, San Francisco, 1989.

Stuckey, M. "Partner with Care (The Concept of Partnering)." *Manage*, 1993, *44*(4), 28.

Tannen, D. *You Just Don't Understand*. New York: Random House, 1990.

Therrien, L. "Retooling American Workers." *Business Week*, Sept. 27, 1993, p. 76.

Vaill, P. B. *Managing as a Performing Art: New Ideas for a World of Chaotic Change*. San Francisco: Jossey-Bass, 1989.

Weiner, E. "New Boeing Airliner Shaped by the Airlines." *New York Times*, Dec. 12, 1990, p. D-12.

Index